GETTING

THROUGH

How to Talk to
Non-Muslims About
the Disturbing Nature of Islam

Citizen Warrior

For more information, sign up for free updates at

citizenwarrior.com

You can write to us at
citizenwarriorchief@gmail.com and
citizenwarriorgeneral@gmail.com

ISBN-13: 978-0615690988
ISBN-10: 061569098X

Proceeds from the sale of this book are donated to the
Tennessee Freedom Coalition.

The leaves on the cover: Where we come
from, every year the leaves of trees start
to fall right around September 11th.

September 11th, 1683, Islamic warriors had invaded
and defeated Greece, Bulgaria, Romania, and Serbia.
They plowed their way through Austria to Vienna, and
were besieging the city. But on September 11th, 40,000
soldiers arrived from Poland to save Vienna. That was
the beginning of the end of the Islamic military conquest
of Europe. That's why Osama bin Laden chose September
11th to strike his blow against the free world.

DEDICATION

This book is dedicated to those who were curious enough to read Islamic texts, and who now want to share what they've learned with their fellow citizens. This often thankless, challenging task is the one most necessary to preserve our freedoms.

CONTENTS

ACKNOWLEDGMENTS

We'd like to thank Andy Miller and the Tennessee Freedom Coalition for their tremendous support and encouragement. We'd also like to thank Bill Warner for his painstaking analysis of Islamic texts.

INTRODUCTION

TALKING TO non-Muslims about Islam can sometimes be enormously satisfying. People are surprised and amazed and walk away from the conversation understanding important new things about the world.

But at other times it can be incredibly frustrating and extremely upsetting. For the sake of our future, you must keep speaking up anyway. This is where the battle will be won or lost — in personal, private, often upsetting conversations. That's part of the price we will pay for freedom.

When you feel upset and your heart is pounding, and you just can't believe your own family member can be so stupid or arrogant or whatever, just remember, this is *war*. It's not a war against your family member. It is an ideological war, and war is unpleasant. You are a warrior and you've got to be brave. Take a deep breath and tough it out. This is what has to be done.

Throughout history, whenever anyone has attempted something truly game-changing, there was *strong* opposition to it. It's hard to believe, but there was strong opposition to the Declaration of Independence, to women getting the right to vote (that fight took 70 years — in the United States!), to establishing and enforcing laws against drunk driving, to gaining basic civil rights for African Americans, and on and on.

If something is good and right and needs to be done, it is not only possible, it is *likely* there will be intense opposition to it. Otherwise it would have been done already.

So *expect* it. Expect resistance. Expect objections. Expect people to argue with you and try to put you down or do anything other than listen to what you're saying. It's part of the sacrifice in this war that you'll have to put up with if you want to make a difference.

You must not return like for like. You must not insult people or get angry at them. You must find a way to remain relaxed.

Think of what you're doing as a kind of "Salt Works protest." Remember the movie, *Gandhi*? If you haven't seen it, you really should.

The Salt Works protest is one of the most powerful scenes in the movie. Gandhi organized a protest against the "Salt Works," a salt processing plant. Britain had an absolute legal control over salt, the most important commodity in India at the time.

The plan was for the protesters to walk up to the salt processing plant, four at a time, and try to walk past the guards in order to claim the Salt Works as India's natural right. When they got in front of the guards, the guards pummeled them with their batons.

The four marchers were knocked down and sometimes knocked out, and fell bleeding to the wayside as four more Indians walked up bravely only to get beaten.

Four by four they continued through the day and into the night, stepping forward with their heads held high, not raising their arms to protect themselves and not fighting back. But not stopping.

They knew they would get hurt, but they also knew it would open peoples' eyes. And it did. It galvanized the world. It showed the British rulers that the Indian people would not accept British dominance any more. Indians were determined to resist British rule until the rulers of Britain saw the truth for themselves that it was time to leave.

The lesson for us here is that you must understand, going into these conversations, that you will get abuse. You must absorb the pain for the sake of freedom, without giving any abuse back, without getting angry or sarcastic, without personal insults, without condescension or bitterness, without defensiveness, and continue to speak the truth until the non-Muslim you're talking to sees the truth for himself or herself.

This is difficult. It may be the most difficult thing you have ever done. And it may also be the most meaningful and important thing you've ever done. Below are some principles and coaching to help give you courage and guidance on this brave endeavor you've embarked on:

1. Talking about Islam is not *necessarily* upsetting. And arguing a point with someone you love is not necessarily upsetting. But arguing about Islam with someone you love *can* be extremely upsetting. But it is worth doing for many reasons.

First of all, it will help motivate you to learn the information very well, and to learn to explain it more clearly. It "ups your game." It makes you take your learning and your articulation more seriously. It is trial by fire. Use that upset to make yourself better, more determined, more prepared, and more informed.

In military training they push recruits to extreme limits. Why? It makes them better warriors.

By the way, throughout this book, we will be using the term "Islam" and "Islamic doctrine" interchangeably because they refer to the same thing. Islam is not someone's opinion. Islam is the sum total of the teachings found in Islamic texts. "Islamic doctrine" refers to the written content of the three books considered sacred by Muslims: The Koran, the Sira (Muhammad's biography) and the Hadith (a large book of anecdotes and quot-ations of Muhammad).

2. Try to see your pounding heart as not necessarily a bad sign. How often do you do *anything* so courageous and meaningful that it makes your heart pound like that? Do not wish your conversation would end. Stay in it and keep educating. It's good for you even if you don't actually change that person's mind — the process helps you increase your ability to handle these conversations; it's good for increasing your skill at articulating points; and it's good for your motivation to learn.

3. Having a conversation in writing (through email or Facebook) is better in some ways than a face-to-face conversation (worse in some ways, too: they both have their advantages). In a written conversation, you can take your time to answer, and you *should* take your time. If you are upset and obsessing about it, don't try to get your mind off it. Print out the conversation so far and read it. Then re-read it and make notes. Look up facts. Write out your responses and edit them before sending. Get *through* to the person. Do your best. Think of it all as *training*.

4. Err on the side of understatement instead of overstatement. You might think that overstatement is more powerful, but in its persuasive impact, it is *less* powerful.

5. Try to be as accurate as possible. Your listener often strongly wants what you're saying to *not* be true. They will desperately grasp at anything you say that they can invalidate so they don't have to accept the disturbing truth. So don't give them anything to grasp onto. Tell the strict truth.

6. Focus on teaching about Islamic doctrine, and how that doctrine is being used today. Always keep aiming your responses back to that one thing. Don't get sidetracked by other political issues. Keep your focus.

7. Be as kind, as forgiving, and as charitable as you can. Don't respond to their sarcasm or condescension if you can help it. Be bigger than that. Answer with facts as unemotionally as you can (except for empathy). Showing empathy for Muslims or empathy for the person you're talking to is a good thing to show. But if you can avoid it, restrain yourself from being angry or upset or intense in any way. Stay relaxed and stick to the facts.

8. Keep your class. Conduct yourself with honor. Take your time and think out your answers so you don't say something you'll regret.

9. Stick to what you know for sure. In writing, back up what you're saying with good links.

10. Do not overwhelm your listener. In writing, do not send a fifteen-page response or a hundred links. Keep it simple and basic. Be selective and use only the best you can come up with.

11. Don't let people divert the conversation onto a topic *they* want to debate. Stay clear on what *you* want to get across and use whatever they say as a jumping off point to get your message across. Make it *your* forum, follow *your* agenda, not theirs. This can be done without seeming obstinate or without the other person even knowing what you are doing. Just keep steering the conversation to what you want to talk about. People will often try to divert the conversation to some other issue because they're "losing."

12. Don't let them get depressed. If you can see your listener is starting to grasp the situation, and maybe feeling depressed, anxious, or upset about their new understandings about the supremacist nature of Islam (all of which are understandable responses), explain to them there are smart people working on this, and some good solutions have already been developed.

But then say, "But of course none of these solutions can happen with so many of us in the dark about Islam. More people need to know about Islam." Turn your listener into an educator. Help them respond to their disturbance with *purpose*. Tie their intense reaction to a motivation to do something about it, and then tie that to the urgent need of more people to know about Islam's prime directive: To establish Sharia law in all nations as the dominant law (we'll go into more detail about this shortly).

13. Think about your task like this: If you don't educate the person you're talking to, she or he will be unwittingly on the side of the enemies of freedom. Personal conversations are probably the only way these people will be reached. Not many politicians have the guts to speak honestly about Islam. Not many mainstream media sources have the guts either.

And most people who don't already know about Islam's prime directive are ignorant because they only expose themselves to sources of information that agree with what they already think. One of the *only* ways they are going to find out is from *you*. Think of it that way and that'll strengthen your determination.

14. Cut yourself some slack. Talking to non-Muslims about the disturbing nature of Islam will be one of the most difficult and challenging things you've ever done. Don't get down on yourself for getting upset about it, for losing sleep over it, or for losing your cool. That all comes with the territory. You *could* keep your mouth shut like so many others do, and you wouldn't have so much trouble. But you're not like that, are you? So accept the difficulty and the challenge. Expect it. And cut yourself some slack when you feel powerful emotions about it. This is serious stuff. Powerful emotions are completely appropriate.

15. Push them to read the Koran. If you can see that your listener is never going to believe you, turn the conversation in a new direction. Focus on *why* they should read the Koran. Tell them about good versions of the Koran, explain why they are good versions, and explain how they should stop listening to anybody's *opinion* about Islam and find out for themselves.

16. When the approach you're using isn't working for a particular person, *use a different approach.* If you keep doing what you've always done, you'll keep getting what you've always gotten. Everybody is different. Maybe an approach that worked well with one person won't work with another. So stay flexible and creative.

17. Read this chapter whenever you're upset by a conversation you've been involved in. That's why I put this chapter first. It's one thing to read this in the comfort of your home when nothing is going on, but when you've had a difficult encounter with someone you love, this coaching will not only make you feel better, it will help you improve your approach for next time, which will prevent you from feeling demoralized or bitter about your "failure."

We need you to stay in the fight. We can't afford to lose anyone. We *must* tell our fellow non-Muslims the disturbing truth about Islam. Nobody else is going to do it. It's up to us. And they must be told in a way that will penetrate their already-existing barriers to listening. Let's get it done.

WHAT GOOD DOES IT DO?

ONE OF THE MOST important things I recommend a citizen do about Islam's relentless encroachment on the free world is *learn* about Islam and *share* that information with their fellow Westerners.

But if you've ever tried to tell your friends about jihad, you've probably discovered that most people don't want to hear it. They will sometimes argue with you even if they know nothing about Islam, and they don't understand why you would want to "bash" another religion.

So the question is: How can you talk to people about a subject they don't want to talk about?

One possible approach is to first *motivate them to listen.*

Almost as a prerequisite for this topic, before you can really have a good listener, you will need to explain why it's important to know more about Islamic teachings. What good does it do? Most people you come across will literally not have a clue why you would even be *interested*, or why they should be.

So here are the top twelve reasons why it's a sane, rational, sensible goal to know more about Islam.

When you start to talk about jihad or Sharia and you can see the resistance or suspicion on the face of your listener, ask them, "Are you wondering why I'm even interested in this?"

If they are curious, let them know about one or two of the reasons below. While you're reading the list here, pick out the ones you think would be the most effective, and make it a point to remember them for your next conversation:

1. Orthodox Muslims are immigrating to Western democracies. From within those democracies, including the one we are living in, orthodox Muslims (believers in the literal truth of Islamic doctrine and Muslims who try to follow the example of Muhammad) are setting up terrorist cells right now. Their spokesmen are delivering fiery tirades at mosques and at demonstrations in our own country, calling the faithful Muslims to rise up against the infidels (you and me), telling the Muslims in their mosque it is their holy duty to overthrow the government and to establish Islamic law.

Orthodox Muslims are recruiting native-born Westerners into terrorist groups and political-activist groups.

They are in free countries now, preaching hatred. And most Western democracies allow more in all the time. Why? Because most Westerners don't know much about Islam.

2. They will perpetually try to change our laws, from within and from without. They have already done so wherever they are. Islam is a *political* ideology. It is the *duty* of faithful Muslims to work toward making every government on earth follow Allah's law (Sharia law).

If Westerners knew what was going on, they could resist it. But our ignorance makes their job very easy.

3. They are having more children than most of us. There are many ways to wage jihad and subjugate infidels. One is through violence and intimidation. Another is through reproduction. Orthodox Muslims are immigrating in large numbers into Western democracies, the men are marrying up to four wives (sometimes supported by their adopted country's welfare programs), having as many children as they can, and teaching them to be devout Muslims.

Orthodox Muslims will try to turn any country in which they live into an Islamic state, no matter how long it takes. They *have* to. It is their religious duty to do so, whether they want to or not.

4. The teenage children of heterodox Muslims are vulnerable to the persuasion of orthodox Muslim recruiters. Even if many of the Muslims who immigrate are authentically heterodox (they would like to ignore the hostile, intolerant parts of the Koran), their children are vulnerable to recruitment as they see through the "hypocrisy" of their parents' incomplete worship.

The children of heterodox Muslims have heard all their lives from everyone in authority that the Koran is a direct message from the Almighty Himself. As teens, if they hear an imam or recruiter tell them what's actually in the core Islamic texts, they will be shocked. The texts contain clear instructions to wage a continual war on unbelievers until the whole world submits to Islamic law.

The teens will look at their parents and feel disgusted. Their parents — the ones who have told them repeatedly that the Koran is the perfect word of Allah — ignore much of the book.

So in other words, it wouldn't even matter if we could somehow screen Muslims who immigrate to Western democracies for fanaticism. Even if we only let in casual, half-hearted Muslims (heterodox Muslims), their children are potential "homegrown terrorists."

And we cannot ignore the added benefit of dying while slaying infidels: They go straight to Paradise and have 72 beautiful wives ready to do their bidding. What 15 year-old boy wouldn't find that an attractive proposition?

All his life he's been told the Koran is Allah's message, and when he finally reads it cover to cover, he will discover those imams were right: It

says quite clearly that if he dies while killing infidels he will go straight to Paradise without passing GO, without having to be judged, and there,
awaiting him, is his lovely harem. And that's the
only way he can guarantee he will get there.

It doesn't take any interpreting or "reading into" the Koran to know what it says. There are no
vague analogies or stories open to multiple inter-
pretations as there are in the Torah, the Bible, the
Bhagavad-Gita, or the Tao Te Ching. The Koran is a
clear, simple, direct message written by one man.
Anyone who reads it will know what to do.

This is why, in a recent study in Britain, researchers found a shocking fact: Second-gener-
ation Muslims are more orthodox (more "radical")
than their immigrant parents.

**5. Confusing current events will become under-
standable.** Once you learn what's really going on,
the tragic terrorist attacks that make you think,
"Why are they doing this?!" are suddenly illumin-
ated, and you know *exactly* why they're doing it,
and why most Westerners don't have a clue about
what's going on.

You would think that learning about Islamic
jihad would make you hate Muslims, but strangely
enough, it does the opposite. Most Muslims are in
an even worse situation than the infidels. The
more you learn about Islam, the more sympathy
you have for Muslims who had no choice in the
matter and cannot escape (especially in Muslim-

dominated countries) without risking their lives and the lives of people they love.

But sometimes learning about the subject is upsetting. It is a *shock* to learn what's in the Koran, knowing that one and a half billion human beings consider this book their most important religious book.

But after you get over the shock, knowing about Islam makes world events *less* upsetting. You will understand what's going on for the first time. You will no longer wonder what the hell is happening in this crazy world. You'll finally understand.

Of all the benefits of learning about Islam, this is probably the one that had the most impact on me. Political events that have been happening since I can remember — all the hostage situations and hijacked planes and bombings — all seemed so unnecessary and confusing. And you can watch the news all day long and get no clarity whatsoever about why these things are happening and what they all have to do with each other. It's a relief to finally comprehend the bigger picture.

6. You can help your fellow Westerners understand. This is a nice benefit of learning about orthodox Islam. Your understanding can help you shed some light and help eliminate the confusion you see in the people you know. It is a gift to the people you know to calm their confused minds. It is a valuable service you can provide your fellow citizens.

7. Your education will be well-rounded. Most of us have some knowledge about Judaism, Christianity, Buddhism, Hinduism, Taoism, and Confucianism. We've heard quotes by their founders, we know some of what they taught, we know a little of their history, etc. But almost every Westerner is ignorant of the most basic teachings of Islam.

So if you are interested in being a generally well-rounded, educated citizen — even if you don't care about terrorism — you should want to learn about Islam.

In addition, of course, is the fact that almost all of the armed conflicts in the world today involve Muslims in one way or another. And almost all terrorism is Islamic and fundamentally motivated by the teachings of Islam, as the terrorists themselves proudly tell anyone who will listen.

8. Your vote on this issue is important. If you vote, you are helping to elect leaders who make legal and political decisions, like how to change the immigration policies, and who to prosecute for trying to overthrow the government. When you understand more about Islam and its relationship to terrorism, you will be able to know which leaders have a grasp on this subject and which do not, and vote accordingly.

9. It is interesting. Once you get over your initial uncomfortable feelings about the subject, you'll find much to hold your interest. Do you know, for example, why Osama bin Laden chose September 11th as the day of his attack on America? Because the last high-water mark of Islam occurred in 1683 on September 11th.

Islam had expanded and conquered for centuries, and was finally stopped at the gates of Vienna when 40,000 soldiers arrived just in time to break the Muslim siege of the city.

Islam's spread was held back by superior military force ever since. Their dominance had been receding since that day. But the new resurgence has set out to finish the goal (the world domination of Islamic law), so al Qaeda chose September 11th to kick off the new era.

Before I started learning about Islam, I didn't know about the gates of Vienna. I didn't know why the Crusades happened. I didn't know why Middle Eastern countries seem so dead-set on destroying Israel. I didn't know what the hijacking of planes and the holding of hostages was all about. I have learned so much, and a lot of it has been very interesting.

10. Knowledge can immunize us. Have you ever gotten what looks like an official email from Amazon or PayPal, asking you for account information? Those who don't know this kind of thing can happen *are vulnerable* to these cons, and might give their personal account information to a criminal.

The email usually says something like, "There has been a problem with your account. We need you to verify your account information or your account will be canceled." And they provide a link. When you follow the link, it looks every bit like the official web site. If you give your information, you just gave your bank account to a scam artist.

If you know about this, if you've heard of the scam, you are immune to it. If you want to check it out just in case, you will not use *their* link. You will type "amazon.com" or "paypal.com" into your browser and go check your account to see if anything is really wrong.

With that little bit of knowledge, you avoided a major catastrophe. Knowledge makes the difference.

It is exactly the same with knowing about Islamic teachings. Once you have a pretty good grasp of what's going on, you're less afraid, less paranoid, and less vulnerable to the tricks orthodox Muslims use to bamboozle ignorant Westerners. When enough of us are educated, they'll find their plans thwarted at every turn.

If you don't know about Islam, you will not be able to tell the difference between orthodox and heterodox Muslims, so you will have to either distrust them all (which isn't cool) or trust them all (which would be stupid). Educate yourself and you won't have this dilemma.

11. Your freedom is at stake. I know that sounds very dramatic and rabble-rousing, but it is quite literally true. All the different factions of orthodox Muslims have a single goal in mind: the dominance of Sharia law. They didn't make this up. They didn't "interpret" their holy books that way. They didn't have to guess. Islamic scholars have been clarifying Islamic doctrine for 1400 years.

These people are not joking. This is not a casual hobby for them. They have dedicated their lives to it. And oil-rich Islamic governments are pouring vast amounts of money into the project.

They won't ever stop. This is a war that has gone on for 1400 years, and as far as they're concerned, it will go on for another 1400 years or as long as it takes to win. Many orthodox Muslims are completely dedicated. They are gaining the advantages of new technologies. They are well-funded. They are highly passionate and dedicated, and literally willing to blow themselves up to kill even a few of us.

Some are actively seeking advanced weapons and are perfectly willing to use them on infidels. It is entirely possible they could gain control of a nuclear or biological weapon.

I don't know how the West will ultimately win this war, but I know this: Until enough of us face and understand what we're up against, we don't have a chance. Cheerful obliviousness will always be easily defeated by grim determination.

12. You'll be ahead of your time. In the future, everyone will know about Islam, either because the whole world will have been subjugated under Islamic law, or because enough of us learned about it ahead of time to successfully defend ourselves against it.

Either way, by learning about it now, you are one of the elite few, the vanguard of a new era.

THOSE ARE THE TWELVE most important reasons someone should want to know about Islamic doctrine. When you begin sharing something about orthodox Islam with someone you know, and you see their eyes start to glaze over, or you see that look in their eyes that seems to say, "Are you some kind of nut?" ask them this question:

> "Are you wondering why I'm even interested in this?"

They will probably nod their head. Then you can share with them why you think it's important. Let them know what's at stake and why this is a fascinating subject to learn about.

Once they are motivated, you can then go on with what you wanted to tell them in the first place.

These one-on-one conversations you have with your friends are the first and most important step in the process of halting and reversing the increasingly dangerous spread of orthodox Islam. People need to be educated, one conversation at a time.

We should *not* be casual about this or approach it in a leisurely way. Right now Islamic terrorists are organizing cells within the borders of your country. Right now orthodox, believing Muslims are building mosques and preaching hatred and the overthrow of your government. Right now they are immigrating to your country and having as many babies as possible. Right now great quantities of seemingly inexhaustible Saudi oil money are being used to build madrassas for the sole purpose of teaching poor Muslim boys nothing but the Koran.

The Right to Believe What You Want

But even after someone understands why it is important to know about Islam, you will probably get a second layer of resistance. Why?

Educated people in Western democracies have a particularly hard time dealing with a conversation that says something negative about another culture or religion. That is almost entirely a good thing. But not entirely. In this case, an exception should be made because generally speaking, Westerners are very unfamiliar with Islam. They don't have any idea what the Koran says its believers should do, and even when they hear someone (like a Muslim terrorist) quote the Koran, they assume that must be incorrect or taken out of context.

When it is *a form of worship* to kill non-Muslims, it is a good idea to make an exception to a blind rule about religious tolerance. When a belief system is intolerant of other belief systems and works to suppress them, it should not be tolerated.

Most Westerners make the assumption that all religions are basically alike. And we have a deep-seated respect for other cultures and the right of everyone to believe what they want. We have a profound distrust of any hint of arrogance or any feelings of superiority for our own culture. It is almost at the level of a taboo.

This distrust is mostly a good thing. It's one of the reasons we are able to have such a rich, diverse society with people of all kinds getting along with each other.

So most Westerners feel pretty strongly that everybody has a right to believe what they want. And they've been told repeatedly that Islam is a religion of peace. That is the source of the second layer of resistance you may get. It's important to know what mindset you're talking to.

A third layer of resistance to talking about Islamic doctrine is the obvious fact that it's a scary and upsetting subject. This makes it somewhat of an unwelcome topic for normal conversations. This ugly, scary quality is compounded by the fact that most people do not think they can do anything about it. Feeling helpless intensifies the feeling of anxiety.

And there is yet a fourth layer of resistance, which is perhaps the most fundamental: People do not want to believe Islam is a warlike religion because if it's true, it seems to imply we will have to go to war with all of Islam to defend ourselves, and that is almost unthinkable. The idea is enough to frighten the most courageous infidel. Go to war with 1.5 billion people?

But of course, learning there are some basic things in the religion of Islam that make it incompatible with modernity or democracy does not mean war with all Muslims is inevitable.

First of all, many — maybe even *most* — Muslims would like to ignore the violent and intolerant parts of Islamic texts, and many of them have been and are now at war with fundamentalist Muslims. The conflicts in Algeria, Iraq, Afghanistan, Lebanon, Pakistan, and Egypt, to name just a few, are mostly heterodox Muslims at war with orthodox Muslims.

So even if an all-out war were necessary, it would not be against *all* the world's Muslims. Not even close.

But besides that, the "war" that really needs to take place is in the minds of our fellow Westerners. Once we are well-versed on Islam, certain precautions will become obvious and will go a long way toward protecting us from danger (such as changing our immigration laws or enforcing our sedition laws).

Just as the knowledge of Amazon or Paypal scams simply and easily avoid what could be a financial nightmare, knowledge of Islam can go a long way toward simply and easily avoiding the nightmare of an Islamic fundamentalist invasion into democratic countries.

Fear of the *implications* of a fact is not a legitimate reason to avoid talking about a fact, anyway, but I thought I would mention it because the fear may well be lurking in the mind of the person you are talking to and make them resistant to hearing anything bad about Islam.

But once you can get over these hurdles and broach the subject, so much can be said that ultimately makes us stronger and less confused, it is worth the trouble.

It is important to help make your listener interested in the subject. Try to make it interesting and don't try to play up the scariest parts unless you feel you have to. Keep getting better at it. This is important work, and we should do it wholeheartedly.

It can do a lot of good indeed to say something negative about Islamic doctrines, if it is done the right way. Memorize the list above, motivate your listeners to hear your message, and then tell them what you know. Your skill and determination in doing this work can prevent immense suffering and ultimately save lives.

Orthodox and Heterodox Muslims

You've heard the terms "radicalized Muslims" and "fundamentalist Muslims." We use those terms to make sure everyone knows we're not talking about "normal" or "moderate" Muslims. There is a good reason to try to make this distinction.

The main reason is because if you say "Muslim," you might mean all Muslims, and clearly all Muslims are not behaving the same and do not believe in the doctrine with equal fervor.

The only piece of information missing from most peoples' understanding is that the "radicalized" Muslims are not really radical. They are orthodox. They are simply doing what it says in their scriptures they are supposed to do. They're not "hijacking" their religion or misinterpreting it. Most non-Muslims are unaware of this.

The first definition for "orthodox" in Answers.com is: *Adhering to the accepted or traditional and established faith, especially in religion.* That's perfect. And it is easily understood by most Westerners. It's a term we're already familiar with.

And in Answers.com, heterodox means: Not in agreement with accepted beliefs, especially in church doctrine or dogma. You can delete the word "church" and that's a great definition for what has been termed "moderate" Muslims. It's accurate and makes the distinction very clear.

So I'll be using the term "orthodox" to describe someone who strictly follows the teachings in the Koran and the Hadith, and who tries — as a good Muslim is supposed to do according to the doctrines — to follow Mohammad's example.

A LESS UPSETTING WAY TO TALK ABOUT ISLAM

TERRORISM WORKS. Islam is the bully of planet Earth. They say we must either join their gang or pay them money and if we don't do what they say, they'll hurt us or even kill us. They mean business. Jihadists will commit suicide to terrorize the world into submission. Sharia law seeks to destroy our democracy and take away our freedom of speech and thought and religion. They mutilate the genitals of their little girls, kill their own wives and daughters to retain their "honor," and keep their women in the position of second class, subordinated sex slaves. Sharia law says it's okay for a man to have sex with girls as young as nine as long as he marries her first. They are taking over the world, infiltrating governments and the U.N., willing to die and kill for Allah, and they've been at it for 1400 years!

Okay, stop for a moment. How do you feel having read that?

It's upsetting for non-Muslims to hear about Islam. The information makes us angry because we can see orthodox Islam encroaching into our lives. This kind of information can make you feel afraid because you see what's happening in places like Europe and you can see the same thing beginning in the U.S. The facts can overwhelm people and leave them depressed and defeated and wanting to give up.

This is my point: When you tell someone a disturbing truth about Islam, you will make them feel bad. This is not good for your relationship. And if you're not careful about how you share this information, you will harm the bonds you have with your family and friends. It happens all the time.

This is the real problem: People need to know what's happening, but we can't count on the media or the government to keep us informed — so we need to connect in other ways. We need our relationships. We need to be joined together to make strong organizations to battle the aggressive encroachment of orthodox Islam.

But talking about Islam is upsetting, so people avoid bringing it up, and even when they do, it often leads to upsets. We end up arguing with each other or avoiding each other or lying to keep the peace. And all these ways of coping with the upset strain your relationships.

Islam drains your time and your relationships just because it is so terribly hard to discuss without getting upset.

But we need to keep talking about it. Everyone must know what is happening. So we keep trying to get through to them even though it keeps causing upsets. Sometimes people actually listen, but often it's just too much for them and if you keep trying, they'll stop talking to you altogether. When you're upset, you prevent the transfer of information.

Jihadis not only blow up buildings, but talking about jihad can cause your relationship to blow up. So what can you do?

First, don't try to share the truth when you're upset. It needs to be shared, but not *while* you feel bad. Nobody likes being around you when you're upset. You need a change of attitude and a better strategy for sharing what you know. You can accomplish both with one thing: When you feel bad, do some good.

If you want to talk about Islam and share what you know, you first must get busy *doing something about it*. You can't let yourself just absorb information. You can't let yourself just watch orthodox Islam's war on the free world unfold. If you don't find something to *do*, the knowledge by itself will destroy your happiness, your dreams, and your relationships.

You must become a citizen warrior and *do something productive* to fight for freedom. Why? Because only in taking an action will you grow strong. Only in *doing* something can you get some relief.

But it doesn't have to be a big thing. It doesn't matter how big of a step you take on. It only matters that you're moving forward.

Go to WhatYouCanDoAboutIslam.com and find something to do. You could join *ACT! for America* or even start a chapter. You could get a conversion kit for your car so you can burn ethanol and stop sending money to OPEC and into the bank accounts of those who fund the global jihad. You could write one letter or send an email asking your members of Congress to co-sponsor the Open Fuel Standard and break oil's monopoly over transportation. You could find out what your child's textbooks say about Islam. It almost doesn't matter what you decide to do. It only matters that you take action.

Taking action does two important things. First, it makes you feel better. Action takes you out of the victim state of mind where this terrible thing is happening to you, and psychologically puts you into the state of being a *cause*, an initiator — *acting upon* rather than *being acted upon*.

This shift from *victim* to *cause* makes a big difference emotionally. Every time you're upset, find a small step you can take. It will bring relief. It will strengthen you. A terrible thing is happening in the world, but there are hundreds of ways to do something about it. You could support women's rights. You could volunteer time to a leader who is fighting the good fight. Look around your world. Look at your family, your kids. What would you do to save the world for them?

The instant you begin, your attitude will shift. You are doing your part. You will feel satisfaction.

You will feel good about yourself. Doing something about orthodox Islam's relentless encroachment will strengthen you and make you feel better.

But the second benefit of taking action is to give you a way to talk about Islam indirectly. Now you can tell people what you're doing. People love to hear stories about what people are doing. They will turn *toward* you, not *away* from you. Then, as you tell them what you're doing, you can tell them *why* you're doing it.

For example: We bought a kit for our car that was pretty easy to install, making our car capable of burning E85. Now we're trying to get more sources of ethanol here locally. When people want to know why we're doing this, we tell them how OPEC controls the price of oil and 40 percent of all money paid for petroleum fuels go to nations who hate freedom and repress and abuse women. And we have stopped giving our money to them.

When you share what you're doing, it is easy to talk about *why* you're doing it. And you're sharing it *as a story* about what you're doing and why. This is a much easier conversation to have. Even if they don't agree with you, it makes for a much less upsetting conversations.

Then, make sure when you talk about Islam that you always couple the information with possible actions *they* could take. Knowledge and action must go together.

So this is the easy way to talk to people about the disturbing nature of Islam: When the truth upsets you, take an action to do some good. When you do something good, share that with people and let them know why you're doing it.

And when you tell them why, suggest ways they could help. Ask them to join you. Always nudge people toward taking an action. Help them take a small step forward. If it makes them feel upset when they hear about the disturbing nature of Islam, encourage them to do a bit of good so they will feel better and, in turn, encourage them to share what they're doing and why they're doing it.

> Hesiod wrote: "If thou shouldst lay up even a little upon a little, and shouldst do this often, soon would even this become great."

Summary:

- Don't share *while* you're upset.

- Take a small action to do some good and you will feel better.

- Share what you're doing and why you're doing it.

- Encourage others to help you or join you. They can share with others and tell *those* people *why* they are taking those actions, and suggest ways *those* people could help.

HOW TO APPROACH A CONVERSATION ABOUT ISLAM

TELLING YOUR FELLOW non-Muslims the disturbing truth about Islamic doctrine is challenging for many reasons. People often have a strong emotional reaction at the mere mention of the subject. But not always.

If you talk to people about Islam, you will get a variety of responses from people. You might have a willing listener who learns from you, or one who listens skeptically, or one who outright rejects everything you say or who won't let you even finish and brands you an Islamophobic racist.

Their response to you depends, in part, on the way you approach the conversation. Not entirely, of course, but your approach can sometimes overcome an already-existing predisposition to respond to any criticism of Islam with hostility.

I suggest you read some of the ideas below, especially before a situation when you know the topic is likely to come up, or where you would *like* to bring it up. Use these ideas as a kind of "pre-game coaching."

We can each do our part to increase the number of people who are no longer unacquainted with Islam by talking to the people we personally know and who already trust us and respect us. For many of them, you are the only one who has a chance of getting through to them. Let's make those opportunities count.

Here are some ideas on how to *approach* a conversation about Islam:

1. Talk about Muhammad.

WHEN YOU ARE talking to your friends about Islamic supremacism, for the most part, they probably won't want to hear it. The topic is scary, political, and you seem to be bashing an "ethnic group." But if you can make your conversation interesting and surprising, that can often overcome their reluctance to listen.

The best way I've found to make introductory information interesting and surprising is to talk about Muhammad.

Most people think the founder of any religion must necessarily have been a peaceful, spiritual, loving person who tried to do good in the world, healed the sick, taught peace, etc. Since Muhammad was the founder of Islam, they assume he must be like that too.

Most people may understand that religious *organizations* can go bad, or *individual* believers can go rogue, but only by twisting and distorting the original teachings of the peace-loving founder.

But as you probably know, Islam is different. And Islam's founder is so different from expectations, talking about him makes a captivating introduction to Islam. Here's the kind of thing I say to people when I'm talking one-on-one:

I have found out some amazing things about Islam — things I would never have thought possible. It's not like other religions. First of all, the founder of Islam, the Prophet Muhammad, led raids on caravans, stealing their goods and often killing or enslaving the people captured in the raid, or holding them for ransom.

He was a political leader and the head of an army, and he ordered assassinations of his political opponents.

He personally ordered and supervised the beheading of over 600 people at one time. That may be the most amazing fact of all. I mean, nobody can imagine Buddha or Jesus doing anything like that!

Muhammad also ordered a rabbi to be tortured to find out where a Jewish tribe had hidden their valuable objects (Muhammad wanted those goods). On Muhammad's order, his men built a fire on the rabbi's chest, burning him badly, and then the rabbi's eyes were cut out.

It is amazing and surprising. At first I couldn't believe it.

And I have not even told you the worst thing. It says in the Koran, in their most holy of books — the book they believe is the direct word of Allah — it says 91 times that Muslims should follow Muhammad's example. In the Islamic religion, Muhammad is held as the ideal man; the one they should emulate.

Most people find all this very surprising. They find it so surprising, I usually follow it up by saying these historical facts are not slanderous libel by Muslim-haters, but historical facts from the books of Muslim *believers*. Muhammad was born in 570 and died in 632. He was a famous figure in his own day, and it wasn't that long ago, so historical facts about him are well-known, well-preserved, and not at all a mystery.

In other words, these are facts about Muhammad that most Muslim scholars and imams know (and accept as true).

After saying all this, you may have frightened your listeners. But you've also opened their minds to something they may have not wanted to hear: Islamic doctrine is unlike other religious doctrines in important ways. Your listeners might not be so quick to silence someone speaking ill of Islam in the future after learning about its founder.

2. Push them to read the Koran.

IT'S NOT very difficult to read the Koran. A child can do it. Many children do it, in fact. With the work they've done at CSPI Publishing making two versions easily readable by Westerners, there is no excuse. The two versions are *A Simple Koran* and *An Abridged Koran.*

The biggest issue facing Western civilization is arguably the relentless aggression of Islamic supremacists, waging jihad by many means, including by gaining concessions, intimidation by violence, and outright murder.

And they continually and openly say they are doing it "in the name of Islam." Islam has only a few central holy books. The most central and important is the Koran.

Non-Muslims need to read this book. Non-Muslims need to be educated about Islam. More than half of the Koran is devoted to how Muslims should deal with non-Muslims.

In the effort to educate my fellow non-Muslims about Islam, I have been experimenting with different approaches. I've been trying to discover what's the best way to get my point across persuasively. One especially effective approach is to aggressively try to sell them on reading the Koran for themselves.

This approach does three good things. First, it reveals that I am both knowledgeable and confident. I'm so confident in what I'm saying, I want them to read the source and decide for themselves.

Second, it brings out in the open the fact that I have read the Koran and they haven't. This gives everything they say the feeling of obvious ignorance, and everything I say the feeling of evident knowledge.

Here's what I've discovered: As soon as I start trying to sell people on reading the Koran and describing what's in it, the whole tenor of the conversation shifts from a kind of arrogant dismissiveness to a respectful openness to what I'm saying. It's magic.

And the third good thing about this approach is that *it's all you would need to do.* If they read the Koran, you no longer need to tell them anything about Islam.

Convince them to read *A Simple Koran* or *An Abridged Koran,* and explain why these are good books. Even your description of these books is a powerful display of your wealth of knowledge on the core subject and their total lack of knowledge about it.

For example, here's what I said recently to a friend of mine. We'd had a brief conversation in person, but it was cut short by circumstances, so I followed up with an email. I wrote:

What I meant to say is that there are good people who are Muslims, but in order to be a good person as a Muslim, you have to be a lousy Muslim (not follow the teachings of the religion). If you don't believe me, you really should read the Koran for yourself. Go to the source, man. It's not hard to understand, and it is not at all vague. It says exactly what it means. There are no clever parables to decipher and no metaphorical prophesies. It is full of straight-up statements written by a single person. Direct. No room for misinterpretation.

I recommend a book called A Simple Koran. *It is simple in the sense that it is made to be understood by Westerners. But it is the entire Koran written in modern English. It is hard to get through the first three-fourths of it (because it is incredibly repetitious and boring) but things really heat up at the end. It will blow your mind. No kidding.*

Don't assume any more, and don't listen to raving maniacs like me any more. Find out for yourself.

In that second-to-last line, I referred to myself as a raving maniac to soften the harshness of accusing him of assuming he knows about Islam when he doesn't.

So anyway, try this approach and see how it works for you. If you haven't read the Koran yet, you really need to do it. Trust me on this. It will put your conversations on a whole new footing. Then after you read it, push people to read the

Koran for themselves. It is probably the best approach I've ever used.

3. Think in terms of small bits and long campaigns.

THE MOST important thing a citizen warrior can do to help defeat jihadis is to educate and persuade everyone in your circle of influence. Educating and persuading is sometimes delicate business, and the people you talk to may have preexisting reasons to reject your point of view before you even finish your first sentence. Because of this, it helps if you think in terms of small tidbits of information. A little at a time. And over a long time.

Opinions are usually changed slowly. Over many months, a person can completely change their opinion about something. But an opinion is almost never changed in a single argument. In fact, one of the best ways to make someone a passionate believer in what they already believe is to make a really good argument against their opinion, mercilessly attacking it with facts.

But a few interesting facts here and there, casually delivered, interestingly presented, can alter a person's opinion over time without them ever thinking they've been influenced. As far as they are concerned, they changed their *own* opinion, and that's the best result you can have.

This makes your task much easier than trying to argue with people, or getting into heated debates. All you have to concern yourself with is *what interesting fact you can share today.*

You get into brief conversations with people all the time. Often they ask you, "What's new?" These are perfect opportunities to mention an interesting tidbit. "I was just reading a book last night by this lady who disguised herself as a Muslim and filmed secret jihadi meetings right here in America. You know what she found?" This is a reference to the book, "Terrorist Hunter."

A statement like that makes a person curious. She will want to know more. Or, if not, no big deal. You've planted a little seed.

I've often started great conversations by saying something like this: "I was reading a book on Muhammad yesterday and I'm totally surprised about something. Muhammad is not like any religious founder I've ever heard of. Did you know he once ordered a Jewish rabbi to be tortured for information about where the rabbi hid some jewels? Or that he personally ordered the beheading of 600 to 900 captives? It's amazing! Can you imagine Buddha or Jesus doing something like that?"

It's a tidbit. It often gets a good conversation going. And even if not, you've added a small bit of information that can change an opinion over time, or make someone more open to information in the future — information she might have deliberately refused to accept before.

Think in terms of *what is interesting*. What is *surprising*? Find good stories and facts that will be interesting for people to hear.

While you're reading or listening to audio-books or watching DVDs, look for juicy tidbits you can share. Write them down.

Think small. Find something you can say in a just a couple sentences. Ideally your conversations would be driven by the other person's curiosity. Say something very short and interesting, and let *them* ask you more about it.

If you have conversations like this with people, over time, some of them will come to think differently about jihad and about concessions to Islam.

4. How to stay calm when talking about Islam.

YOU KNOW what it's like. You're in a discussion, and even though you're making some good points, you don't feel satisfied with your conversation because you're getting too worked up. You can feel your own upsetting feelings take away from your message. You want to do better.

Below are a few things that will help you feel more relaxed during these conversations. This will help get your message to penetrate.

a) Don't try to "win the argument." Ideally, do not even *think* of it as an argument. Think of your role as one of telling someone something surprising and interesting that they didn't know. The goal of "winning the argument" will make you too high strung.

Scale down your goal and you will instantly feel calmer. Aim for something more reasonable and attainable: Aim to get a little solid information across, so the other person is a little more informed about Islam after the conversation.

Think in terms of small bits and long campaigns. This will help keep you calm and increase your ability to persuade. Oddly enough, people are more persuaded by calm understatement than by intensity.

b) If the other person makes a surprising argument or asks a surprising question that throws you off, think of that as something *useful*. Think of it as something to pursue — either to find out more about it so you're better informed for the next conversation, or think more about it so you will have a good response next time.

If you go into a conversation with this attitude — the attitude that you'll learn the most from the most difficult conversations — you'll be less flap-pable. You'll stay genuinely calmer.

c) Know a lot. This really helps you stay calm. If you know you have much more knowledge about Islam than the other person — if you are well-versed in Islam, if you've read the Koran, if you've listened to audio material many times, if you've studied the answers to objections (which you will find in the next chapter) — it's fairly easy to stay calm, no matter what they say to you. It will all be "old hat" and you'll easily be able to answer any-thing they come up with.

d) Be clear ahead of time about what you think are the three most important points to get across. Do the same kind of preparation people do for television interviews. That is, keep your primary message in mind, and use whatever the other per-son says as a jumping off point to get your mes-sage across.

Figure out what three points are most impor-tant, and really work on them. Become knowledge-able about those points. Figure out good ways to present those points. And then when a conver-sation on Islam comes up, try to transition your conversation to a place where you can make at least one of those points.

There's nothing magical about the number three. In a conversation, you may not be able to get all three across. Maybe just two or even one, depending on how much time you have. But the principle here is to have a few points, a very few points, already decided and prepared ahead of time.

e) Aim to be calmer and more reasonable than the person you're talking to. Be the better person. Make no personal jabs, don't use sarcasm, don't raise your voice, don't raise the pitch of your voice or sound hysterical, etc. Make them admire the way you're handling yourself. You can do this if you aim for it. If you want to *win*, let it be winning in this: That you conducted yourself with more class than the other person.

f) Don't overgeneralize about the person you are talking to. Their overgeneralizations about *you* are an important part of what gets you so upset in conversations. The second you open your mouth to express your point of view — as soon as they know what your point of view *is* — they've put you into a box that you probably don't actually fit into, and that box sometimes prevents you from getting through to them, and it's frustrating.

Be better than that. Don't do this to people. If you can restrain yourself from overgeneralizing, it will make your conversation easier. Don't set yourselves up as two opposing viewpoints if you can help it. There is undoubtedly a lot you two agree about.

Don't put the other person in a box, even if they've done it to you. The person may not be as one-sided as you assume or as unreasonable as you expect.

g) Take time off from the counterjihad movement. Relax and take care of yourself. Take care of your close relationships. You've got to be in this for the long haul and not burn yourself out.

h) Stay in good communication with several people who *support* what you're doing, who understand how important it is, and who believe and admire your willingness to fight.

It is a psychological boost to hang out with people like this. Find people of like mind on Facebook and friend them. Gather together a posse. Join your local *ACT! For America* chapter and go to the meetings.

It is incredibly encouraging to see and talk to people who understand what's going on.

USE THESE PRINCIPLES to help you stay calm and relaxed during your conversations about Islam. Remember this chapter, and refer to it right before a conversation about Islam, or right after. Learn to make these ways of approaching conversations your natural way of dealing with conversations. You will find you can really *enjoy* these conversations, and if you're enjoying them, you will be more persuasive without even trying.

5. Approach is the key.

I'VE BEEN practicing for a long time, trying to hone my ability to educate people one-on-one about Islam, and I'm pretty good at it. I rarely get into a "debate" or argument, and in fact, it's usually an enjoyable conversation.

I've written a lot about how to talk to people about Islam, but I decided to try to think of all the things I *take for granted* about my approach that I *haven't* written about, and I ended up making the list below.

These are personal rules or states of mind or ways of thinking about these conversations that help them go so remarkably well:

a) I try to only talk to someone about Islam when nobody else is around. I don't want to get into a *public* debate. When people talk in the presence of other people, they are more likely to try to "win" or look good, and less likely to listen and learn. Being in a public situation tends to encourage people to take sides.

Perhaps even more importantly, when someone makes a pronouncement to several people, they find it more difficult to change their mind

later than when they make the same pronouncement to only one person.

All in all, you will be more likely to really in-
form someone one-on-one with no audience.

b) I try not to approach it as a debate at all. I
am careful about the way I *open* a conversation.
And careful about the way I speak, so it becomes
clear that I know what I'm talking about, and that I
know a lot more about the subject than the person
I'm talking to, but I don't do it in a condescending
way. I do not try to "dominate" the conversation
except that I try to establish my authority by
saying something simple like, "Have you read the
Koran? No? Well, when I read it the first time, I
was really surprised to find..."

c) I try to keep it *interesting* for the listener. I
want them to find out something they are surprised about and interested in.

d) I don't try to rub their nose in it. I don't try
to *make* them get how scary and horrible it all is. I
realize because I've been learning about Islam for
a long time, things that no longer shock me still
shock the hell out of others. I don't need to try to
scare them. Even the mildest parts of this topic
scare most people.

e) I try to keep it casual. "Hey, did you hear
about what happened in France? They banned the

burka. Yeah, and it was almost unanimous..." I try to prevent giving the impression I am on a campaign to stop the Islamization of the world. I'm just talking about interesting things I've learned lately. I try to maintain a feel of easygoing conversation, and sometimes it becomes very engaging.

f) I deliberately stay relaxed, and try to "curb my enthusiasm." And I keep my sense of humor. This topic is intense enough without adding to it by being intense myself. I pause when I'm talking and ask them questions, and I don't give them the most shocking things until they are already fairly well-versed about the less shocking things.

g) I do not let it appear as if I want them to change their minds or that there is any kind of conflict between us. I find common ground. I try to speak about things I know they will care about, like the human rights angle or women's rights, or whatever.

h) I think in terms of small bits and long campaigns. I know I keep mentioning it, but it's a good one and I didn't want to leave it off this list. It's important. I don't try to get the whole educational process done all in one conversation. I let it happen in small pieces over many months to give them a chance to absorb it and think about it, and hopefully ask me questions about it later. I plant seeds and expect the dawning realizations to happen over time rather than expecting enlightenment overnight.

I assume there will be many already-existing beliefs they hold that will need to change for them to understand more. Sometimes changing beliefs produces an internal struggle, and forcing more information into a struggling mind can make the person not want to talk to you any more. Plant the seeds and be patient.

i) I sympathize with their resistance and disbelief. I was there once, too, and I know it's a shocker when it starts to really sink in. I remind myself of how I felt when I first started learning about Islam. I didn't want to believe it. I didn't want to put any attention on something so negative.

Remembering my own frame of mind helps me empathize with my listener, and I think that helps the communication process.

j) I try to make it clear to my listener that we are on the same side of this issue. I know a lot more about it, but we are both non-Muslims. We're on the same team.

I convey the feeling that we don't have all the answers and we're exploring this topic together. If the person brings up a good point or a counterargument, I will either say "that's interesting" and think about it and then come back later with more information, or I will say something like this: "I used to think the same way. But when I found out..." And I lead them further into the topic with more information.

k) I reframe their objections like a salesman. Sales training manuals will often tell you to be *glad* when someone raises objections, because it means the person is interested. People who are not interested just make excuses and disappear.

Someone who is arguing with you is often presenting arguments they think *other* people might bring up to see if you have a good answer for them — an answer that would satisfy other people. They do this because they are interested in believing you, but want to be sure.

So I don't feel put off by questions or arguments or "objections." I see it as a sign of interest and curiosity, and I try to answer the objection in a way that gives more information (rather than in a way that makes the other person feel wrong or stupid or anything negative). This perspective on objections helps prevent me from interacting in a confrontational way. It helps me avoid turning the conversation into some sort of contest or disagreement.

l) When I have a difficult conversation and it really bothers me because I didn't have a good response, I find a quiet place and write out what the other person said as soon as I can. I do it on my computer. Then I separate out each statement the person made and write out the answer I *wish* I had made at the time. I print it out and read it. All of this tends to make me less upset about it when I think about the conversation.

If my "failure" continues to bother me, over the next few days I may occasionally read over what I wrote out and add more to my answers and print up the new version. I look up facts if I am unsure about something. I write it all out until I feel I've made a really good answer.

If you do this, you will be better prepared for the next conversation. Does this seem like a lot of effort over a five minute conversation? It is in these small conversations where the whole thing will be won or lost.

I welcome these difficult conversations, because I know I will use them like this. You should welcome the times when you're stumped and you don't know what to say. It can deepen your understanding and make you grow.

13. I try to never use the words "Islam" or "Muslim" by themselves. I always say "heterodox" or "orthodox" before every one. Most people know at least one Muslim person and cannot, out of the goodness of their heart — out of personal loyalty or just plain human empathy — think of that person as having bad intentions, and they know that not all Muslims are devout. So if you give blanket statements about Islam or Muslims, they reject

your statements for perfectly sound reasons. Always use the descriptors.

6. What to Do About Those Who Oppose Your Educational Efforts.

YOU'RE TRYING to educate your fellow non-Muslims about Islam. And people argue with you. They defend Islam, even when they don't know anything about it. And if there are any Muslims around, they will usually tell you "true" Islam is peaceful, etc. Unless you've read the Koran or studied a lot about Islam, these reactions are confusing and sometimes disheartening.

I want to straighten out the confusion, so let me first describe our situation. We've got people who *call themselves* Muslims who don't know much about Islam and haven't read much of Islamic doctrine, and yet they identify themselves as Muslims because their parents were Muslims. So they defend Islam when it is criticized.

Then we've got the orthodox Muslims who do not want non-Muslims educated about Islam because it interferes with their political goal of bringing the whole world under Sharia law. They try to stop non-Muslims from discussing Islamic doctrine in any way they can, including arguing, accusing them of racism or "Islamophobia," and they will use deception (taqiyya), threats of violence, riots, and even murder to silence people.

Then we have non-Muslims who do not know much about Islam but are blindly committed to the (usually) admirable principle of multiculturalism, and who don't want to see any group slandered or criticized unfairly. There are a lot of them in the West, and many of them will actively defend Islam against criticism.

That is a lot of opposition to what we're doing. You will see that the common theme to all three of these groups is *education*. The orthodox Muslims are already educated about Islam, and they are committed to its goals. The Muslims in name only are not likely to listen to a non-Muslim telling them what Islam is about, since they think they already know. A large proportion of the multiculturalist non-Muslims will not listen to anyone because they are also sure they already know.

But there is a proportion of non-Muslims who know little or nothing about Islam *and are curious*. Those are the ones we should concentrate on.

This is salesmanship 101: Try to find "qualified prospects" because if you waste half your time making sales pitches to people who don't have the authority to make a decision, or who don't have the money to buy what you're selling, you're not going to make a lot of sales. You're wasting far too much of your working day. You've got to focus on *qualified* prospects only. It's just more efficient.

Your "qualified prospects" are those who have the following characteristics:

1. They are in good rapport with you. They like you.

2. They respect what you say.

3. They don't already have their minds made up about Islam.

4. They don't know much about Islam.

5. They are curious about Islam.

6. They are non-Muslims.

Notice that the people we talked about earlier — the orthodox Muslims, the Muslims in name only, and the committed multiculturalists — do not qualify. If you have *nothing else* to do and nobody else to talk to, go ahead and tell any non-Muslim in your vicinity about the terrifying brilliance of Islam (unless it's your boss and it will get you fired, or some other practical reason to keep silent). Why not? Something might stick. But if you have a choice, focus your efforts on the most qualified "prospects" you can find.

7. Casually Talk About News — And Then Make a Good Point.

IN A COMMENT on one of our blogs, someone going by the name of "Western Feminista" left the following description of what she does to educate her fellow non-Muslims. This is an intelligent and creative approach:

"I have generally had the most success with using articles in the news, and mentioning things casually...one great example was when a Muslim lady was sentenced to six months jail for *falsely* accusing a policeman of forcibly removing her veil. I agreed that it was terrible that she had been sentenced and explained that "man-made laws" are not recognized by Muslims, so really, she had done nothing wrong in perjuring herself and making a false complaint...the people I was speaking to couldn't believe what I was saying, and it gave me the ideal opportunity to explain Sharia law to them — something that they had no knowledge of before.

"The right to wear a burka has been another situation — citing the above case again, the woman claimed that it was impossible for the policeman to prove it was her as she had only her eyes showing, and so she should not have been in court.

"Again, I agreed that in fact, we should all be able to wear a balaclava to enter a bank, shopping center, or government office — the government has no right to make me recognizable in any instance.

"The people I was speaking to suddenly began arguing *against* my rights to do that, and I was able to speak about other concessions to Islam that have been recently made — again, things that they had not thought 'important' were suddenly placed in a context where they became very important.

"Hopefully other instances will come up, and I can keep getting the message out there, slowly and gracefully."

I asked Western Feminista if I could publish her comment, and she said yes. Then she emailed me *more* intelligent ways to educate our fellow non-Muslims:

"Another example I have used is regarding the illegal asylum seekers arriving here, and rioting in our detention centers (I am from Australia). So many people are of the opinion that we should accept them immediately (to stop the rioting) as we have much to spare, and have prided ourselves on accepting immigrants over the years.

"I agree, citing the wonderful way that the Italians, Greeks, Vietnamese, etc. have assimilated into Australia, and how they enriched our country ...and isn't it unfortunate about the Global financial crisis at the moment that is making it so difficult for governments to be able to afford to give as much as in the past? Especially as there are so many Muslims that really seem to want to make Australia their new home, and how they may actually become a majority in the future...it's not an unreasonable assumption, really. I haven't had anyone dispute it yet.

"Then I ask them how much they would be willing to pay per month so all the Muslim asylum seekers could be released immediately into the community. $50? $100? $200? Of course this brings looks of disbelief, or a small token amount is mentioned...I then casually mention that it would be like paying jizya — and am always asked to explain in more detail...no one has ever heard of it, and it scares people to think that it will hit them where it hurts — the wallet.

"I suppose you could call it *Islamic Education by Stealth* (lol)."

This is excellent. She has obviously thought about what she was going to say and *how* she was going to say it ahead of time, and presented her information for maximum impact and surprise. With enough of us doing this kind of thing, we might see a change in public opinion about Islam in short order.

8. How to Stay Relaxed and Feeling Good While Talking About Islam.

WHEN I WAS in high school, I remember my friends and I making the observation that when we didn't have girlfriends, girls didn't seem interested in us, but once we had a girlfriend, suddenly interested girls were everywhere we turned. And we knew why: Because we no longer felt we *needed* a girlfriend. We didn't have that anxious mood about us any more. If girls liked us, that was fine with us. And if they didn't like us, that was fine with us too, now that we had someone who liked us a lot. We were confident, self-assured, and relaxed. And therefore, appealing to girls.

The same principle applies to talking about Islam. If you can find a way to not "need" someone to believe you or agree with you, they are more likely to believe you and agree with you.

So if you find yourself getting somewhat upset during conversations about Islam, I suggest you change the way you think about it so if someone agrees with you, that's fine with you. And if they don't agree with you, that's fine with you too. But I mean *really* fine with you (rather than trying to convince yourself it's fine, even though you are actually upset).

Find a way to think about it so you feel good about it however the conversation goes.

How can you think about it so you have that kind of relaxed confidence? Experiment with different perspectives and see what works for you.

For example, I have convinced myself that I am on "the leading edge" and that eventually it will become common knowledge that the doctrines of Islam are not peaceful but intolerant, politically domineering, and violent. Over the last thirteen years of writing for the Citizen Warrior blog, I have seen good evidence that my assumption is true: More and more non-Muslims are waking up to the truth about Islamic doctrine.

Since that's the case, any *particular* individual I'm talking to doesn't really matter in the long run. If they believe me, I have gained one more recruit to our side. If they don't believe me at the moment, they will eventually learn the truth, and they'll remember I'm the one who told them first. I know this is a little silly, but this perspective works for me. It helps me feel less anxiety about whether they are convinced or not. This helps prevent me from getting upset, and makes me more persuasive.

Here's another perspective I have deliberately cultivated: There are already a whole bunch of us who have educated ourselves about Islam. In other words, *I already have a girlfriend.* Of course, being Citizen Warrior, I am in communication with a lot of people who share my understanding of Islam. But anyone can find plenty of like-minded thinkers by reading the comments on Jihad Watch articles, joining a counterjihad Facebook group, going to *ACT! For America* events, etc.

You can easily expose yourself to an almost unlimited number of educated counterjihadists who share your understanding of the situation. And when you do, it will help you feel less alone, isolated, or "needing" anyone's approval on this topic.

And another perspective I cultivate is a trust that if things get worse — if we can't reach enough people fast enough — it will only cause more people to open their minds to the facts about Islamic doctrine. There was a strong movement in the United States against getting involved in "Europe's war" until the Japanese bombed Pearl Harbor. Then suddenly the majority of Americans completely changed their opinion.

You might be thinking: 9/11 didn't suddenly change everyone's opinion. But it did wake up many of us, and we're waking up the rest. And every new atrocity orthodox Muslims commit causes more of us to awaken, so even if I completely fail to convince anyone in a one-on-one conversation, I have planted the seeds of understanding, and as events unfold, they will come to understand, so it's not a dire necessity to convince them immediately.

These perspectives help me stay relaxed in conversations, and that makes me more persuasive. I'm sure these are only a few of the many possible perspectives that might help. Experiment with yourself and find what works for you. Try on different ways of thinking about it until you find some that help you enjoy the process, and help you reach people more effectively.

9. Reveal the disturbing truth a little at a time.

THE DAY after Osama bin Laden was killed, I was talking to a friend of mine at work. He is a dedicated multiculturalist who hopes what I've been saying about the Koran and Islam isn't true. We were talking about the news, and I quoted Osama bin Laden: "We love death. The U.S. loves life. That is the big difference between us."

My friend looked baffled as to why bin Laden — or any human being — would say such a strange and horrible thing. And this just confirmed for him that bin Laden was an animal, a cruel murderer who would have been a murderer no matter what religion he was.

But then I said something that I could tell really caught him. I said, "Well, it's a sentiment Muhammad expressed. He said unbelievers love the life of this world better than the hereafter, and because of that, they are rejected by Allah. A lot of Muslim leaders have said the same thing in pretty much the same words as bin Laden — Nidal M. Hasan, the Ayatola Khomeni, hell, it's even the Hamas motto!"

My friend looked like I just jolted him with a Taser for a second. He knows I've read the Koran twice, so he took what I said as a shocking *fact*.

I don't like to make people squirm, and I wanted to give that indigestible tidbit a little time to integrate into his worldview, so I went on about my business as if nothing happened. It was just a casual remark, a simple matter of fact, and my demeanor revealed no more than that. But I have the feeling he stayed up late that night thinking about it. I think he might come around.

I feel sometimes like a therapist helping someone gradually come to terms with a painful memory that they subconsciously fear to remember.

Years ago I read an account by Milton Erickson — a psychiatrist and innovator of hypnotic techniques — doing an experiment in a college class he was teaching. One of Erickson's students couldn't stand the sight of blood. This was a problem because he was studying to be a doctor!

Erickson hypnotized the young student and uncovered a memory he had completely blocked from his conscious mind. But rather than overwhelm the student's conscious mind, Erickson gave him post-hypnotic suggestions to allow the memory to be revealed to his conscious mind slowly, bit by bit, over the course of many weeks.

I sometimes operate the same way with information about Islam. For some people, to discover that the core doctrines of Islam — a religion in which 1.5 billion people claim membership — teaches intolerance, totalitarianism, and violence, is not only overwhelming and frightening, it is profoundly disruptive to their worldview.

So if I am going to have regular and continued contact with a particular person, I reveal the information *gradually.*

Just a little at a time does the trick. Let them come to it on their own terms. As Dale Carnegie says in his book, *How to Win Friends and Influence People* — a book every counterjihadist should study — when trying to change someone's mind, it's best to let them think it was *their* idea, and the gradual approach is one way to do that.

10. Discuss the Movie, "The Kingdom."

I WAS TALKING to two men I was working with (who don't know I am involved in the counterjihad movement — I had never worked with them before). I said, "Have you guys seen the movie 'The Kingdom' with Jamie Foxx?"

One of them said, "I've seen part of it." The other guy said he hadn't seen it. "It's a really good movie," I said, "other than the ending, which really pissed me off."

They looked at me curiously, so I said, "Well, the movie is about a terrorist attack in Saudi Arabia. You know how they have enclosed compounds there for Americans to live in — Americans who work there?"

They both nodded.

"In the movie, there's a baseball game inside one of these compounds, with lots of people there, enjoying a sunny afternoon with their families, and these terrorists drove up and started shooting into the crowd, and then a suicide bomber dressed as a policeman walked into the panicking crowd and blew himself and everyone else to smithereens. Then when the first responders showed up, the terrorists set off a truly enormous explosion, killing even more people."

"Back in the United States, Jamie Foxx is an FBI agent, and he's talking to a bunch of his fellow FBI agents, giving them a briefing on what happened. One of their agents was on the scene in Saudi Arabia — one of the first responders — and died in the blast. When Jamie says this, one of the women agents in the front row of this briefing room starts to cry, but Jamie Foxx walks over to her and whispers something to her, and she stops crying.

"So the movie goes on, and the FBI agents go to Saudi Arabia, and eventually track down the mastermind behind the bombing and near the end of the movie, the old mastermind gets shot, and he's dying, and his grandson is hugging him and crying, and the old man whispers something and the grandkid stops crying.

"At the end of the movie, we find out what Jamie Foxx whispered into the FBI woman's ear and what the old terrorist guy whispers into his grandson's ear. They say the same thing: 'Don't worry, we'll kill them all.'

"And that's what pissed me off," I told these guys, "because when the FBI agent said that, he meant, 'We're going to kill all the bad guys who participated in this brutal slaughter of our good friend,' but when the terrorist mastermind dude said it, he meant, 'We're going to kill them all — all the Americans, all the infidels.' The movie tried to imply that they were the same. And that just irked me."

One of the men I was talking to, the older one, said, "You know, there's only the tiniest difference between Judaism, Christianity, and Islam," and he said this like it was something we all knew, and this was only the preamble to something else he was going to say, but I interrupted.

"There is actually an enormous difference between them. I'm only saying this because I have just finished reading the Koran. And although I know Muslims like to *say* they're all very similar, Islam is very different in important ways."

The other one who hadn't spoken much, a young man, looked curious, like he wanted me to say more, so I said, "Yeah, you would expect the founder of a religion to be a certain way, and Muhammad, the guy who founded Islam, was not at all what you'd expect."

The older man said, "He was a warlord!"

"Yeah," I said, "he ordered the assassinations of people who criticized him, he personally took part and oversaw the beheading of over 600 people in one night. Actually it took a couple days. And he knew a group had hidden treasure, so he tortured a rabbi for information. He had the rabbi tied down and they lit a fire on his chest to get him to talk. I mean, this is just not the kind of thing you'd expect from the founder of a religion. But you have to admit, it explains a lot!"

They both nodded. "The bad news is that it says in the Koran — their most holy book — it says 91 times that a Muslim should use Muhammad as an *example*. They're supposed to *imitate* him."

This is sobering information, and it came like a wall of reality, hitting them like a big, fast-moving wave, and there was a good reason to change the subject, so I did. I got in a few really strong facts with very little resistance.

Hopefully we'll have more conversations, or they will be curious and try to learn more. But whatever happens, they are very likely to never hear that line the same way again — the line that "the three Abrahamic religions" are similar to each other. And they won't be so quick to believe someone who says Islam is a religion of peace. They'll have doubt in their minds about that. And when legislation comes around that encourages cutting off money to Saudi Arabia or stopping Muslim immigration or preventing a mosque from being built at Ground Zero, they will be less likely to dismiss it out of hand.

This is the kind of brief conversation happening all over the free world between non-Muslims. Slowly but surely, we're informing ourselves.

Like the passengers on Flight 93 (the flight that fought back on 9/11), we're sharing with each other what information we can gather, and the reality of our situation is collectively beginning to sink in.

11. Mention this: People who criticize Islam need bodyguards for the rest of their lives.

THERE ARE A FEW points I think we should try to work into our conversations with people about Islam:

> 1. Anyone can freely criticize Christianity, Judaism, Buddhism, Hinduism, Scientology, Jainism, atheism, and every other "ism" on the planet, but not Islam.

> 2. People who criticize Islam (like Geert Wilders, Salman Rushdie, Ayaan Hirsi Ali, etc.) need bodyguards for the rest of their lives. People who criticize Jesus or Joseph Smith or Krishna or any other religion or political ideology don't need bodyguards.

> 3. And Islam is the only religion trying to assure everyone else that they are a religion of peace. You don't see the Amish

trying to convince anybody how peaceful they are.

I think it's possible that these simple facts, stated plainly and matter-of-factly, at an appropriate time in the conversation, would sink in and do their magic. And one morning, your listener will wake up and declare, "I think maybe Islam isn't really a religion of peace!"

And we'll have one less dhimmi in the world. One less person who unwittingly aids the enemy. One more ally when ALAC laws (laws that disallow any foreign law from being applied) are being voted on or when immigration policies are being changed. One more person who will support a politician willing to speak honestly about Islam.

Islam is the only religion that makes it necessary to acquire bodyguards for the rest of your life when you criticize it. Sink that tidbit into your friend's mind and watch what happens.

ANSWERS TO OBJECTIONS

BELOW IS a list of responses you are likely to get when talking about the terrifying brilliance of Islamic doctrine to someone who knows little about it. What follows is kind of like sales training.

When you get a job as a salesperson, the trainer will usually teach you about the most common objections customers have, and will teach you how to handle them. Then when a potential customer gives you one of those objections, you won't be thrown off; you will have a competent and well-thought-out answer — an answer that will satisfy the person making it.

But maybe even more importantly, you'll give an answer that will satisfy the person your customer will talk to later. In fact, the objection may only be what your customer thinks others will ask later about his purchase.

People often make a response that they think *other* people might make. This is true in sales, and it's true when you're talking about orthodox Islamic doctrine.

If your listener accepts what you're saying about Islamic doctrine, and then they go share what they've learned with a friend of theirs, what objection might that *friend* come up with? Your listener will probably wonder about that, and might bring up that objection to see if you have a good answer for it — a persuasive answer, a satisfying answer, an answer that would even convince their skeptical friend.

If you have a good enough answer, you can go further into the conversation with a willing listener. If you don't have a good enough answer, the conversation could stall and maybe stop, and your listener's mind might close.

Not many people really want to hear about Islamic doctrines, at least at first. It's ugly and it's scary. But if you do well enough in your conversation, you can get some good information into the other person's brain, and we will all be better off. This is the most important thing that needs to be done right now: *Successful* one-on-one conversations between people who know about Islamic doctrine and people who don't.

But people often respond negatively. The good news is that the number of possible negative responses you get is *limited*. There aren't an unlimited number of things people will say to you. The possible responses are limited enough that you can prepare for them.

People will often present their responses as if that's the end of the argument. Case closed. As far as they are concerned, they just gave the final word on the subject.

But if you have a good answer, the conversation can go on, and can go deeper, and your listener will walk away more informed about Islam and less confident in what they believed they knew. That's one less potential dhimmi in the world; one more potential recruit to our side.

So below are possible answers to the likely objections you will hear:

1. "But it is just a small minority of extremists."

In other words, you'll be talking about Islam and what it says in the Koran, and they'll come back with, "You're talking about a *minority* within Islam."

This is the biggest misconception people have — that Islamic supremacists are terrorists and they're small in number and a fringe group, and that the vast majority of Muslims are peaceful, law-abiding, kind-hearted, religiously-tolerant believers in humans rights. How can you respond? Here are a five different ways to answer:

Possible response number one: Even a small minority of 1.5 billion people is still a lot of people. And the minority is not nearly as small as people like to think. Yes, the number of Muslims following Muhammad's command to "kill unbelievers wherever you find them" may be small, but a much larger percentage believes in the political *purpose* of Islam and is working toward that goal in other ways besides killing people.

There are many ways to wage jihad. Violence is only one, and not a very good one in many respects. Demographics is another (that is, moving to a new country, maybe even letting them support you with welfare, but definitely out-breed the original inhabitants, build up a politically active and powerful voting block of orthodox Muslims in that country, and then start pressing for concessions to Islam — pushing to make the existing culture yield to Islamic standards, one concession at a time).

Many forms of jihad are already being used — litigation jihad, forest fire jihad, falsify-textbooks jihad, infiltrate security organizations jihad, and the list goes on and on. *Violent* orthodox Muslims may, in fact, be the *least* of our problems.

Possible response number two: You mean the ones who are blowing themselves up in order to kill non-Muslims? Or flying planes into buildings? Or trying to get their hands on a nuclear bomb so they can set it off in downtown New York City? Those are worthy of concern, but in the longer term, the Muslims waging jihad by other means may be more dangerous. (Of course, at this point, they'll probably say, "What other means?" and you have opened up another opportunity to educate them further.)

Possible response number three: In orthodox Islam, jihad is obligatory for *all* Muslims. Jihad doesn't mean *warfare*. Jihad means *to struggle* in whatever way you can to achieve Islam's single political goal: The subjugation of all non-Muslims to Islamic law. That political goal is a Muslim's religious duty. Expending effort to achieve it is a form of worship. According to Muhammad, it is the *most important* form of worship in Islam.

Muhammad didn't approve of meditation or navel-gazing. He said the way you can prove your devotion to Allah is by *action*. So a lot of mainstream "moderate" Muslims are active, constantly working toward the end-goal of worldwide Islamic dominance. Some of them do it by paying their zakat, which goes to the mosque, which goes to supporting Muslim causes (which are almost entirely political causes).

And they do it by having lots of children, to give Muslims a demographic advantage in democratic countries. They do it by making every non-Muslim they meet think that Muslims are harmless and well-meaning and Islam is one of "the three Abrahamic religions."

They also do it by crying "racism" every time someone criticizes Islam, even though they know full well Islam is not a race (they say it because it gets the desired response: It shuts people up, gets people fired, discredits the speaker, and ruins careers). They do it by writing to television or radio programs that portray Islam in an unflattering light, demanding apologies.

It is *all* jihad. Bamboozling the non-Muslims is jihad. As Muhammad said, "War is deceit." And as you can see, they have been winning the war. Most non-Muslims know almost nothing about Islam and yet have a feeling that it must be a perfectly fine religion.

Possible response number four: We get that impression (that it is a small number of extremists) because almost none of the constant attacks by jihadis are covered in the media. If you go to the web site, thereligionofpeace.com, you will see every verifiable attack in the world made in the name of Islam. There are about five attacks a day. Some big, some small. But it adds up to a constant war being waged against all non-Muslims everywhere in the world simultaneously.

More people are being killed in the name of Islam *per year* than were killed in the entire 350 years of the Spanish Inquisition in the name of Christianity. And each one of the jihadis doing the killing is supported by a network of Muslims that, while they are not killers themselves, help to make it happen, help to finance it, help to hide them, feed them, encourage them, and protect them. The ones committing violent jihad are only the tip of the iceberg.

The ones committing violence may be a small number, but many more Muslims are following Muhammad's example and waging jihad on many fronts and at many levels at once.

Possible response number five: The Muslim Brotherhood is the largest Islamic organization of any kind in the world. That makes it *mainstream*. Not fringe. The Brotherhood's goal is to make the whole world submit to Islamic law. And they are actively (and in many ways successfully) accomplishing their goal.

Most of them do not advocate random bombings, which are strategically ineffective in most places and counterproductive to the goal of world domination.

They have a long-range plan and they've been putting it into effect for over twenty-five years. This is not guesswork. Their documents have been seized in FBI raids. One such raid led to the prosecution of members of the Holy Land Foundation.

The Muslim Brotherhood has established lots of "legitimate" organizations in the United States, which work toward the goal of destroying our government from within (this is the Muslim Brotherhood's stated goal) — CAIR, MSA, ISNA, NAIT, etc.

There are organizations that raise money to promote jihad (while fooling people as to the real purpose of the money), organizations that sue on behalf of Islam, organizations that recruit on campuses and turn non-Muslim students against America, organizations that influence how textbooks in American schools portray Islam, organizations that influence how the FBI deals with Muslims, organizations that fund and control madrassas and mosques all over America and make sure they teach hatred, intolerance, and reverse-integration. And more.

And they do it all under our noses because our attention is focused on the hot-headed jihadis who blow things up.

OKAY, NOW YOU HAVE five possible responses to the objection, "But it is a small minority of extremists." Read over these responses and pick the one you would most want to use, and remind yourself of it every day until it comes to mind naturally. Let's prepare ourselves for these conversations so they can go well. People who aren't yet acquainted with Islam *must be reached!* It is up to us. Let's get it done.

2. "My friend is Muslim and he's really nice."

Sometimes when you're talking about Islam, someone will tell you something like this: "My cousin is married to a Muslim man and he's a really great guy." And they will say it like that's the end of the argument. They pronounce it as if their statement obviously cancels and disproves everything you've said about Islam. Here are some possible responses:

Possible response number one: I can see that you are defending your friend, so let me be clear that I'm *not* attacking your friend or anyone who calls himself a Muslim. I'm talking about Islamic *doctrine.* I'm talking about what a devout Muslim is supposed to do according to their prophet, Muhammad, and what millions of Muslims in fact do.

Possible response number two: Is he a practicing Muslim or a Muslim in name only? If he is a practicing Muslim, jihad is *obligatory.* But keep in mind, jihad means struggling toward the political goal of the dominance of Islamic law. Violence is only one of many ways to work toward that political goal. Also, if he is a practicing Muslim, he can't be friends with you, according to the Koran. He can *pretend* to be your friend if it serves the goals of Islam, but if he actually feels affection for you and really considers you a friend, he is doomed to burn in hell. You must not have read the Koran yet. I recommend CSPI's version, written for modern English speakers...

Possible response number three: That's good (that he's a really great guy)! But the Muslims following the doctrine still need to be stopped, and one very important thing that needs to happen in order to stop them is for non-Muslims to be educated about what's in the Koran and the Hadith.

Our fellow non-Muslims ought to be made aware of the game plan of the enemies dedicated to destroying our way of life. If you are trying to stop people like me from educating non-Muslims about Islam, you are unwittingly helping Islamic supremacists with their political goals.

Possible response number four: Maybe this Muslim's apparent goodness is only *taqiyya*. Another possibility is that he is simply ignorant of what his religion requires of him. I will tell you what is in the Koran, but only if you promise not to tell him. We don't need any more Muslims to awaken to the requirements of their faith. Let him live in benign and peaceful ignorance.

Possible response number five: He's a Muslim and he's really nice? Good! It's entirely possible he does not follow the whole teachings. However, does he pay his zakat (alms)? If so, he is probably contributing to Islamic supremacists who are following the whole teachings (the zakat usually goes to the local mosque, and most mosques in the U.S. are owned and run by dedicated Wahabbis, who are fundamentalists).

Does he pray five times a day? Does he fast for a month during Ramadan? Has he read the Koran? If he had to choose between Sharia law and the

U.S. Constitution, which would he choose? Do you have any idea?! Or are you simply saying your cousin is married to a Muslim with good people skills?

Possible response number six: The existence of a nice Muslim does not invalidate the statement that Islamic teachings advocate intolerance and violence toward non-Muslims. The fact that you know a Muslim who knows how to get along with non-Muslims does not mean he would not also advocate imposing Sharia law on non-Muslims, and does not mean he is not actively striving toward that goal. The fact that he is really nice does not mean he repudiates the supremacist nature of Islamic teachings. The existence of a Muslim who happens to be charming does not discredit a single thing I've said.

Possible response number seven: Is your friend an apatheist (apathetic about his own religion)? If so, I think that's great. But I wasn't talking about people who *call* themselves Muslims but do not follow the doctrine. I'm talking about the actual Islamic doctrine — what it says in their holy books and what nearly all the Islamic authorities have decreed for the last 1400 years — and that is now being followed faithfully by Muslims all over the world. Those who are following the teachings of the Koran and who faithfully follow Muhammad's example are a danger to the free world and a danger to all non-Muslims, and they must be stopped.

Possible response number eight: Muhammad Salah was a very nice man too. But he was also the leader of the worldwide military wing of Hamas, a brutal terrorist organization!

In the book, *Terrorist Hunter: The Extraordinary Story of a Woman Who Went Undercover to Infiltrate the Radical Islamic Groups Operating in America*, Rita Katz wrote about being at an IAP conference in Chicago. That's the Islamic Association for Palestine. There were lots of booths at the conference for "charitable" organizations, and at one of these booths, Katz met a man she already knew about: Muhammad Salah. She pretended she didn't know who he was, and he introduced himself as a "Muslim human rights activist."

Katz, a non-Muslim woman dressed as a Muslim, wrote, "He was small, thin, nearly bald. Totally harmless looking."

He told her these conferences were so important because "we can teach you about the oppression and sufferings of Muslims in America and all over the world."

Then he told Katz his story. He had been a Palestinian with American citizenship, a used-car salesman working in Chicago when he went to Israel to "visit family and friends." But in Israel he was arrested by the Israeli authorities and thrown into prison for five years!

Katz looked appropriately appalled and asked why in heaven's name would they put him in prison? "Because the Israelis oppress innocent Palestinians," he said. "And do you know what is the most shocking part? When I returned to the U.S., after I was tortured and I thought I was going to die in that prison, the Americans placed me under investigation and froze my assets! Me, an innocent citizen, a car dealer, a family man, father of five!"

To any other American citizen, this probably would have been a convincing story. The poor, oppressed Muslim! It's just *wrong* to treat people that way. Those Israelis must be very cruel. Those Americans are so oppressive to Muslims!

But Katz was not an ordinary citizen. She researched people like Salah for a living. She knew all about him.

This frail, innocent-looking man was the leader of the worldwide military wing of Hamas. When he was arrested in Israel he had a hundred thousand dollars in cash on him.

In his testimony, he admitted the money was supposed to go to "members of Hamas's military wing." He displayed detailed inside knowledge of Hamas's structure and funding, and his testimony was later used as evidence in the New York trial of Musa Abu Marzook, the leader of the political bureau of Hamas (and the man who had appointed Salah to his position as leader of the military wing).

Katz writes: "Salah disclosed (in his testimony) that he'd been authorized by Marzook to recruit individuals for training in the uses of explosives to fight in the 'holy war.' In the United States, Salah began training ten such recruits, three of whom were chosen to carry out attacks. In addition to supervising the building of bombs, explosives, and remote detonation devices, Salah was instructed by Marzook to develop biological and chemical weapons for Hamas."

When Nasser Hidmi was caught trying to detonate a bomb in Israel, he said he had been chosen by none other than the poor, innocent, abused, oppressed Muslim, Muhammad Salah.

This is an example of *taqiyya*, the principle of religious deception. According to mainstream Islamic doctrine, Islam is in a permanent state of war with any non-Muslim government that opposes the rule of Sharia law. And in war, deceit is a legitimate tactic.

In other words, as long as it helps the Islamic goal of making the whole world submit to Sharia law, it is perfectly all right to lie and deceive.

When I was trying to figure out what I would choose as the three most important things to tell a non-Muslim about Islam, taqiyya was one of the three. The use of taqiyya is the main reason most non-Muslims are so confused about the real nature of Islam — they are constantly being intentionally deceived by Islamic supremacists posing as reasonable, "moderate" Muslims, who are successfully fooling everyone from political leaders to the media that "Islam is a religion of peace" and that "Islam has been hijacked by extremists."

What they don't want non-Muslims to know is that Islamic teachings are highly political and it is a Muslim's religious duty to strive to accomplish Islam's primary political goal — the establishment of worldwide Sharia law — in any way he can for his whole life.

Why wouldn't orthodox Muslims want non-Muslims to know this? Because they can make better headway if most of us remain in the dark.

3. "What you're saying is racist."

When you're talking to non-Muslims and you say something unflattering about Islam, most Westerners will try to defend Islam. They tend to see what you're saying through the filter of "racism" or "bigotry," and toward such things they have an automatic response: Protect the poor abused Muslims from hatred and fear-based reactions.

They may envision lynchings. They don't want to see racial profiling. They don't want to have internment camps like the Japanese suffered during WWII.

Since they see your criticism as bigotry or racism, they are unthinkingly and reflexively opposed to a perfectly normal and legitimate activity in a free country: Political and religious criticism.

One of our most treasured guaranteed rights is the right to critique the doctrines of any political or religious group. The fact that it might be offensive to someone is exactly *why* free speech has to be protected (if it didn't bother anyone, there would be no need to protect it).

Hopefully you are not a bigot or a racist, but whether you are or not, racism has nothing to do with criticism of Islamic doctrine. Islam is not a race or an ethnic group. There are Muslims of every race. And there are more non-Arab Muslims than Arab Muslims.

If you find racism abhorrent, whoever balks at your criticism of Islamic doctrines and thinks you are being racist actually *agrees* with you, and you should make your agreement on this issue crystal clear.

In fact, we can emphasize the racial issue as an important reason to solve the "Islamic encroachment" problem as soon as possible. Let me explain.

Many people in the counterjihad movement think it will take a dirty nuke going off in Chicago or Paris before the free world wakes up. But after a tragedy or a major attack, people will be angry and afraid, and decisions under those circumstances aren't always the sanest decisions. In times like those, people can overreact.

They do things like put Japanese citizens into internment camps. That was a fear-based over-reaction, and it was bigoted and racist.

We can avoid that kind of overreaction if we talk about Islam *now,* in calmer times.

In other words, talking about Islamic teachings now can help *prevent* racism and bigotry by making sure everyone understands what Islamic teachings are about, and that everyone understands Islam is a *doctrine*, not a race.

This is a point you should stress when someone resists talking about Islam and who seems irrationally *against* talking about it. They are probably afraid you're a bigot. They might be afraid even talking about it with you somehow condones racism.

Make it very clear right up front you're against racism, that Islam is not a race, and that conversations like these will prevent racism in the future if something disastrous happens. If racism is what they were concerned about, you will suddenly have their attention.

If those who are *not* racist think criticizing Islam is racist, *it proves the point.* Namely, that it is vital more people understand Islam.

In other words, if you think criticism of Islam is racist, you are demonstrating that *you* don't understand what Islam is, and you are illustrating exactly why we need to talk about it and learn about it, because if *you*, who are so strongly against racism, think Islam has something to do with race, then how are *racist* people going to react if a nuclear weapon goes off in downtown Houston and kills a million people?

What Do You Call It?

When someone says some of the passages of the Koran are violent, and that Islam itself is political, what do you call that? It's an important question.

It is *religious criticism*. But it's more than that, because Islam is not merely a religion. Islam is also a political system with political goals. So instead of racism or Islamophobia, we could call it religious or political criticism.

But if you call it that, there isn't anything wrong with it. In a free society, it is a perfectly legitimate activity to criticize religious doctrines and political systems. It's okay, for example, to point out that the Catholic church frowns upon birth control, or that Marxism and free enterprise are incompatible.

So when someone explains the political ideology contained in the Koran, it is a completely fair, appropriate, respectable activity, and anyone who calls it racism or Islamophobia either doesn't understand what they're saying, or, more likely, they are trying to censor the person. That kind of censorship is out of line in a free society.

The fact that exponents of orthodox Islam will not tolerate criticism of Islam *is one of the main criticisms of Islam.* The fact that the Koran itself is adamant about disallowing any criticism of the Koran (and calls for a death sentence for doing so) is one of the most legitimate things to criticize about the ideology in the Koran.

If someone doesn't hire a Muslim simply because the applicant is a Muslim, that is discrimination, and that's a different issue. If someone beats up a Muslim *because* he's a Muslim, that is a hate crime and is illegal, immoral, and should be punished.

But criticism of Islamic *doctrine*? It can and should be done. Criticism of the political actions or philosophies of orthodox Muslims? It can and definitely *should* be done.

Explain the Difference

When I'm talking about Islamic teachings and someone says, "That seems racist." I usually respond that I'm talking about the *teachings*, not a person, and that it couldn't be racist anyway because Islam is not a race, etc.

I make the point that: "Even if I were to say, 'All Muslims are evil,' that's not racism, either. It would be an overgeneralization, but it's not racism. If I said, 'Asians are bad drivers,' *that* would be racism."

If I said the tenets, recruitment practices, and indoctrination techniques of the Ku Klux Klan are dangerous to civil rights in America, would anyone call my statement "racist?" Would it be called "hate speech?" Am I suffering from Ku Klux Klanophobia?

No. My statement that the tenets, recruitment practices, and indoctrination techniques are dangerous to civil rights is a legitimate statement of debate, and there is nothing the matter with stating it openly and talking about it.

But say the same about Islamic texts in mixed company and there is an almost audible gasp and an embarrassed silence, as if you had broken some sacred taboo.

Why?

Orthodox Muslims themselves have been accusing their critics of racism and hate speech and Islamophobia, and they've influenced the mainstream media to do the same, so it has entered our mainstream cultural thought-process. Now, it is an almost automatic emotional reaction.

Orthodox Muslims have been using these accusations because they know in the West we have a hot-button on those issues. Nobody wants to be considered racist.

Orthodox Muslims use this fact as a weapon.

So we need to carefully and effectively explain to everyone why criticism of Islamic doctrine is quite different from hate speech, Islamophobia, or racism.

Make this distinction clearly and persuasively. People need to hear about Islam, but as long as they have this barrier to their listening, you can't get through.

4. "Aren't you being religiously intolerant? People in this country have a right to worship as they please. Isn't religious tolerance one of our most important principles?"

Almost everyone in the free world firmly believes in the principle that people have a right to worship as they wish. Even people who are avowed atheists will defend this principle. So to hear anyone (*you*, for example) criticize any religion will naturally offend the sensibilities of people who know nothing about Islam (but assume it is one of many similar religions).

The negative reaction to your criticism of Islamic doctrine can be even more pronounced if they are a believer in another religion because they hear your criticism of orthodox Islam as a threat to the *freedom of religion*, and they will often defend Islam on that basis alone.

How can we respond to this objection? Here are some ideas:

Possible response number one: I am actually *defending* religious tolerance. What should you do with a religiously intolerant religion? What can you do with a religion that will try to stop, defeat, undermine, and even abolish all other religions? If you want to preserve religious freedom, you had better keep the aggressive, intolerant religion on a tight leash. You had better be aware of what they are doing, and you'd better prevent them from getting their hands on the reins of power or it will be the end of religious tolerance for everyone.

Possible response number two: There are two aspects of Islam. One is religious and the other is political. The religious part has to do with fasting and prayer. The political part has to do with subjugating non-Muslims, working to establish Sharia law in places where it isn't already established, and repressing the rights of women.

Orthodox Muslims do not believe the religious part is separate from the political part because according to the Koran and the example of Muhammad, they are *not* separate.

But some people who call themselves Muslim are perfectly willing to violate the tenets of Islam and separate the two. They only want to practice the religious aspects of Islam, which is private, and I have nothing against that at all. I think they have every right to do that.

But others are more orthodox. And it behooves those of us who might be on the receiving end of their political actions to be aware of the political goals of Islamic teachings. Those teachings impact non-Muslims and restrict human rights for Muslim women, and that should be prevented.

In many places in the free world right now, Muslim women do not enjoy the full rights of freedom because those areas are politically controlled by orthodox Muslims, who never let up on their relentless push for political and legal power.

There are areas in Britain, France, and Germany where Sharia law is legally practiced. The governments have given in to Islamic pressure.

In the USA, orthodox Muslims are influencing American textbooks, misleading students as to the nature of Islam and the history of violent and aggressive Islamic expansion. This is a breach of the separation of church and state, it is an example of Islamic supremacists' tireless political aggression, and we must not allow it. We wouldn't allow it for any other group; we must not allow it for Islam.

This is not a suppression of religious freedom. It is a repression of unfair, one-sided, freedom-denying political practices (carried out as a religious duty).

Possible response number three: After the Protestant Reformation, and after many years of persecutions and wars, Britain established a new policy which is the root of our model of religious tolerance today. Any religion or sect could worship as they chose without fear of persecution by the government or anybody else.

Churches that had once enjoyed a monopoly resisted this new policy. They were intolerant of other religions. So Britain told them: You will be tolerant of other religions or you will not be allowed in this country.

If you think about it, this is the only way religious tolerance can exist. You cannot allow an aggressive, intolerant religion free reign. It will try to gain a monopoly. Oddly enough, you must be intolerant of intolerance in order to have tolerance.

Right now 75 percent of the mosques in America are preaching hatred toward non-Muslim Americans according to the Mapping Sharia Project, which sends trained people into U.S. mosques to see if they are calling for jihad. This is a dangerous religious intolerance. It doesn't work to have a situation where everyone allows everyone else to worship as they wish except one group who will only tolerate their own religion. That's the definition of supremacism and it is a threat to freedom of religion.

Everyone has to abide by the principle of tolerance or it doesn't work.

So being critical of Islamic supremacism and stopping its relentless aggressive encroachment is, in fact, an essential goal if the freedom of religion is to survive.

5. "Christianity is just as bad."

When you criticize orthodox Islam, a very common response you'll get is something like this: "Christians do the same thing. Look at the Inquisition. Look at the Crusades. More people have been killed in the name of Christianity than all other religions combined."

A simple way to answer the objection is: "Today, more people are killed in the name of Islam *every year* than were killed in the entire 350 years of the Spanish Inquisition." Direct your listener to see how many people are being killed daily in the name of Islam at the website:

TheReligionOfPeace.com

Memorize that URL so you can recommend it (a similar URL — ReligionOfPeace.com — goes to a pro-Islam site). Write down the right web address for them. The site documents every verifiable act of jihad in the world where at least one person is killed.

The obvious answer is: "The violence in Christian texts does not make violence in Islamic texts okay."

Another answer is: "In the 1400-year history of Islam, 270 million people have been killed in the name of Islam. No other religion even comes close. *Communism* doesn't even come close. Nazism doesn't either. The reason we don't know this is that orthodox Muslims have infiltrated the textbook publishing business in America and have massively edited the history of Islam for Western students. They also heavily influence the Western media."

I once wrote a more thorough article about this issue because it comes up so often. Here it is, entitled *Why I Am Worried About Islam But Not Christianity*:

FIRST LET me say right up front: I am not a Christian, a Muslim, a Jew, a Hindu, or a Buddhist, and I never have been. But whenever I talk about Islam to people here in America they almost always bring up Christianity. They compare Christianity with Islam, basically implying that I am criticizing Islam but Christianity is just as bad. Even *Christians* say this to me.

People who know nothing about Islam try to defend it because they think of Islam as the underdog (an impression orthodox Muslims have carefully cultivated), and good citizens everywhere instinctively want to defend any group (especially an underdog group) against discrimination.

While Islam looks like other religions Westerners are familiar with — Judaism and Christianity — and portrays itself as such, it is profoundly different in important ways.

In response to my statement, "Islam makes the attainment of political goals a religious duty," somebody said to me recently, "Christianity is a political religion too." Below is my answer to him:

"Plenty of people in America and Europe are already aware of the political dangers of Christianity, and have long ago taken steps to prevent it from taking over governments.

"In contrast, very few people in America and Europe know about the dangers of Islam, and, in fact, people are so reflexively against Christianity, they tend to *favor* Islam and give it the benefit of the doubt. When I talk to people about the most basic principles of Islam, I am often shocked at how little people know about this religion.

"Some Christians have political goals, just as some dog fanciers have political goals.

"But Islam is different in an important way: Muslims have *a religious duty* to work for political goals — it is a form of devotion and worship — and Muslims don't get to choose what goals they should strive for; the goals have been decreed by Allah. Muhammad was against living in monasteries or living a contemplative life. The way to show devotion to Allah is to fight for Islam. Literally (and politically)."

As far as I know, no Christians have expressed any desire to kill me. And it would have no doctrinal support from the New Testament if they had.

Many jihadis have openly expressed the desire to kill all Americans, many Americans have already been killed by them, and they have plenty of doctrinal support from the Koran to justify this killing.

There are many dramatic differences between Christianity and Islam. A Christian can leave Christianity any time they want. The penalty for leaving Islam is death.

When Christians kill, it can only be in *spite* of Christian teachings. When a jihadi kills, it is likely *because* of Islamic teachings, and they will tell you so openly and proudly.

Christians sometimes push for the spread or protection of Christian ideas. Jihadis push to do away with hard-earned freedoms and replace the laws of free countries with a repressive, backward system (Sharia law). It is a religious duty for a Muslim to relentlessly strive for the establishment of Sharia wherever they are. Allah considers "man-made" governments (democracies, for example) to be illegitimate. The only legitimate laws are Allah's.

Christian morality insists they tell the truth to all people. Islam's morality insists they tell the truth to fellow Muslims but lie to non-Muslims if it can further the political goals of Islam.

In battle, Christians will try not to kill innocent bystanders. Jihadis don't believe any non-Muslim is innocent and they deliberately kill ordinary (non-military) citizens.

Christians voluntarily try to follow Jesus's example, and he was peaceful and kind. Muslims *must* follow Muhammad's example (it says so 91 times in the Koran) and Muhammad raided his enemies, stole from non-Muslims, held captives for ransom, raped his female captives, owned slaves, tortured people and murdered people.

For sinning, Jesus advocated forgiveness. For sinning, Muhammad advocated stoning and beheading.

Jesus encouraged his followers to turn the other cheek when people criticized him. Muhammad encouraged his followers to *assassinate* people who had criticized Muhammad or Islam. Several people who had criticized Muhammad or Islam were killed by Muhammad's followers with Muhammad's consent and approval. One was even assassinated at his *request* for the sin of criticizing Islam.

According to Christianity, the guaranteed way of getting into heaven is to believe Jesus died for your sins. According to Islam, the only way for a man to *guarantee* his passage to heaven is to die while killing for Islam.

These points I'm making about Islam are not a twisting of Muhammad's teachings; they are not an "interpretation" of Islamic doctrine. Muslim scholars and imams would agree with my statements. This is all based on mainstream Islamic theology.

Those are the main reasons I am more worried about Islam than Christianity. I used to think Islam and Christianity were very similar, but they are not. Why is Islam so different? The reason is historically interesting.

All other major religions were started within an already-existing state. Islam is an historical exception to this rule.

Any organized government will, of course, put a stop to violent uprisings of a rebellious political group. Christianity arose within the Roman Empire, for example. If Christianity had been a militant or political uprising — if Christianity had tried to take over the government — Rome would have killed or imprisoned its followers. Probably many military or political religions did start up then, but we've never heard of them. They couldn't get off the ground.

But Islam arose in Arabia when there was no central ruling power. The whole area was made up of individual tribes. Under those circumstances, the most efficient way to gain converts was by force. And that's how Islam's militancy came to be.

Muhammad borrowed many ideas from both Judaism and Christianity, and that's why it bears a superficial similarity to familiar religions. But it is fundamentally different. The circumstances of its time and place of origin led to teachings that were written down and declared sacred, and those teachings now guide 1.5 billion people.

Muhammad's life itself is an example of the principle that when you don't have power, you dare not use violence. When Muhammad first started Islam, he was one man with little political power surrounded by many others with their own religions and lots of power. He could not be belligerent, he couldn't threaten anyone, so he used *persuasion*.

In the first half of his career, using his persuasive skills, he gained 150 converts. In the second half of his career, he used violence and terror more and more as he gained numerical and financial strength. Using the "conversion by the sword" method, he gained *tens of thousands* of converts in the same amount of time.

Converting by force is a more effective method if you can get away with it, especially if you can reinforce it with total control of the government and the law.

Muhammad created a complete system that rules every aspect of life. But in order to make the system work, Islam must be the law of the land.

It doesn't work, for example, to cover all your women so Muslim men are not sexually tempted by their bodies and faces if half the women in the country are not Muslims and walk around in mini skirts. For the system to work, *every* woman must be covered. And for *that* to happen, the government has to follow Sharia law.

Muhammad used force to gain converts, and all his decrees and justifications for his actions were written down in the Koran, which are now memorized and studied by orthodox Muslims — many of whom take the teachings to heart. The result is an insistent, unrelenting push for the dominance of Islamic standards everywhere in the world.

6. "Not all Muslims are terrorists."

When you talk about Islam, people often respond as if you've made some sort of mistake, as if you are equating a few crazy terrorists with all 1.6 billion Muslims in the world, when "everybody knows" most of them are peace-loving people.

This is an easy objection to answer, but it is also an opportunity to give your listener a deeper education on the subject. Here are a few ideas about how to answer this objection:

Answer number one: Terrorism is only one of many ways to wage jihad. There are at least ten types of jihad (I recommend you find a good list online of the different kinds of jihad and memorize the list). In Islamic teachings, there are five pillars of Islam, five things every Muslim should do. But according to Muhammad, jihad is more important than any of them.

It is a religious duty for each Muslim to struggle for the establishment of Sharia law everywhere in the world. That is jihad. Some do it with bombs. Some do it with immigration and fecundity. Some do it with relentless political actions (waging jihad by gaining concessions). Some do it with "mainstream, moderate" Muslim organizations that try to undermine Western governments.

So in other words, I agree with you completely that not all Muslims are terrorists, but I disagree with you that this somehow implies orthodox Islam's political goal is something we can safely ignore.

Answer number two: That's true, not all Muslims are terrorists, but most terrorists are Muslims, and they kill in the name of Islam. Do you know why? Do you know what they're after? (When they say something like, "Yes, they want the West to stop interfering with Islamic affairs," you can answer with a lesson on Islam 101): Since the beginning, Muslims have waged a war of expansion, and they have tried to justify their violence as a response to a grievance. That's the way Muhammad did it, and he's the example all Muslims are supposed to follow.

Answer number three: That's true, but most Muslims believe Muhammad is a good example to follow. Do you know anything about Muhammad? Knowing about Muhammad explains a lot of what otherwise is incomprehensible in world events. (Here you can tell the story of Muhammad's rise to power and the change in the Koranic revelations. Talk them into reading the Koran.)

Answer number four: The Muslims who are terrorists are able to do what they do because of a tremendous amount of support from their community, and that support is motivated by Islamic teachings. It is also motivated by the hope that the supporters will gain entry to Paradise.

According to Islamic doctrine, the martyr can plea to Allah (once he arrives in Paradise) on behalf of up to seventy of his relatives to get them a ticket to Paradise. For someone who believes Islamic doctrine is true, this is a potent incentive to help any of their relatives who plan on killing non-Muslims.

In other words, that "small percentage" of Muslims who are active terrorists are only the tip of the iceberg of a tremendous amount of popular support for the killing of non-Muslims.

Remember the jubilation throughout the Muslim world when thousands of non-Muslims were killed on 9/11? Only 19 hijackers did it, but clearly many Muslims supported it. Why? Because that's the kind of thing Muslims are *supposed* to do according to the Koran and the "perfect" example of Muhammad.

7. "We can't go to war with 1.5 billion Muslims!"

This objection is not usually spoken out loud, but it's a central fear lurking behind much of the resistance you get when you talk about Islam.

When you're talking to people, you want them to accept the simple fact that Islamic teachings are very straightforward, and they call for intolerance and violence toward non-Muslims and an unrelenting effort to make us all submit to Sharia law.

They'll put up every objection they can think of because they don't want to accept this premise.

If they articulated their fear, it would sound something like this: "For God's sake, that *can't* be true, because it would mean we would have to go to war with 1.5 billion Muslims, and we can't do that!" Some people actually say it out loud.

Like many of the objections, this one is a great opportunity to insert a little more information into a brain that is likely almost entirely empty of any facts about Islam. Here are some possible responses you can give:

Answer number one: Luckily, we don't have to go to war with all of them. Most of the people who are now Muslims never chose to be so. Their ancestors were almost all *forced* to be Muslims. The whole country was conquered and Sharia law was imposed. Sharia puts pressure on everyone to be Muslim, and not just in name only. Under Sharia law, it is illegal to skip the five prayers a day or skip fasting during Ramadan or skip paying zakat (alms to the mosque). In other words, the practice of Islam is enforced by law, so after a few generations, it would be hard to think outside of being a Muslim, especially when the penalty for leaving the faith is death.

But what this means is that many Muslims would choose to live their lives without the constant domination of Islam if they had the option. So even if it came to war, we wouldn't have to go to war with 1.5 billion.

Answer number two: What would you go to war to do? I mean, why would you think a war would be necessary?

Answer number three: We don't need to go to war, we only need to change some of our own laws and some of our own foreign policies. And sometimes we wouldn't even have to change them, we would only need to start *enforcing* them. For example, it is against the law to try to overthrow the government or to even plot to do so. It is sedition. It's already against the law. And yet in three-fourths of the mosques in the U.S., jihad is being preached.

Jihad is the struggle to bring the law of Allah to every person on earth. Another way to put it is to make everyone on earth submit to Sharia law. This goal is an essential element of Islam. It is a core tenet. This isn't some fringe teaching that nobody cares about. This is a primary goal of Islam according to Islamic texts.

If we want the orthodox Muslims in our country to stop working to undermine and overthrow the government, we will have to make a distinction between the political aspects of Islam and the religious aspects, and we'll have to stop people from committing sedition. We do not need to go to war. We only need to educate enough non-Muslims so that no more politicians ignorant of Islam are voted into office. The one thing that needs to happen is *education*. Do you think education is a bad thing?

Answer number four: The problem is not with Muslims, so we don't have to go to war with them. The problem is not even with Islamic doctrine. Our problem is the abject ignorance of the majority of non-Muslims. Because of this ignorance, the West is conceding its freedoms to the constant pressure of orthodox Muslims.

It's like dealing with sociopaths. I found thousands of comments on an online article about sociopaths. Most of the commenters are victims of sociopaths, and they tell their stories about what happened to them — they were conned out of their life savings or they were married to someone who abused their children or one of their parents deliberately drives them crazy, etc.

But two of the people who commented are themselves sociopaths, and their comments illuminate an important principle.

The point of view of most of the victims is that they don't understand how sociopaths can be so mean or cruel or heartless.

The point of view of the sociopaths is that they don't understand how normal people can be so naïve as to trust everyone, so foolish as to never protect themselves from someone who has already proven to be dangerous, or so stupid as to sign over the deed to their house!

The same thing can be said about most non-Muslims dealing with orthodox Muslims. Okay, so it is a Muslim's duty to strive for the political goal of establishing Sharia law throughout the world by any means necessary. But we don't have to *allow* it! They are only making progress toward their goal because *we let them*. We trust them. We make treaties with them. We allow them to immigrate. We make assumptions about them (they must be just like us, they have the same goals and values as we do, their religion must be similar to other religions we know of, etc.) — assumptions clearly contrary to the evidence.

We are *conceding* our freedoms. We are forgoing our own self-preservation. We are voluntarily giving away our ability to defend ourselves.

The problem is not with *them*, it's with *us*. We don't need to go to war. We need to stop being naïve, and that can't happen until more people know about Islamic doctrine.

Most of the people commenting on that sociopath site said they were surprised to find out there was even *such a thing* as a sociopath. The phenomenon of "everyday sociopaths" is not very well known. People know about psychopathic serial killers, but most people don't know there is such a thing as people walking around in ordinary lives who have no empathy for others and cannot develop it, people whose only goal in life is to win and dominate, people who feel no pity or remorse and who have no emotional conflict or guilt when they are cruel.

Some people who told their sad tales in the comments were married to a sociopath for *years* without ever realizing such a person as a sociopath could exist, so they were totally frustrated, anguished, and confused by their spouse's behavior, and of course, in their ignorance they made one stupid, self-defeating mistake after another.

The free world is doing the same thing with Islam's relentless, self-serving aggression — making one stupid, self-defeating mistake after another.

The stupidity must stop. The only thing missing is enough people who have at least a passing familiarity with basic Islamic teachings.

8. "Are you an Islamophobe?"

In Robert Spencer's book, *The Politically Incorrect Guide to Islam*, he quotes somebody else's long definition of "Islamophobia," which includes "attacking the entire religion of Islam as a problem for the world." And then Spencer writes:

> *Does labeling as "Islamophobic" the practice of "attacking the entire religion of Islam as a problem for the world" mean that it is also Islamophobic to focus attention on the Koran*

and the Sunnah of the Prophet as motivations
for terrorist activity? If so, then jihad terrorists
worldwide are themselves "Islamophobic," for,
as we have seen, they routinely point to jihad
passages from the Koran and Hadith to justify
their actions.

In other words, if I say Islam is a political religion that mandates intolerance and violence against non-Muslims, that makes me an "Islamophobe." But it also made Osama bin Laden an Islamophobe.

Islamophobia is a misleading term, as I'll explain in a minute, and yet it is used with great seriousness by governments all over the world, in the media, and by the United Nations.

But "Islamophobia" is a made-up word. It isn't tenable, plausible, or convincing once you really look at it. Using the term is merely a way to slander those who have legitimate concerns about the implications and consequences of the teachings of Islam. It is a way to prevent legitimate criticism and debate about an important global problem. As the historian, Victor Davis Hanson wrote:

> *There really isn't a phenomenon like "Islamo-*
> *phobia — at least no more than there was a*
> *"Germanophobia" in hating Hitler or "Russo-*
> *phobia" in detesting Stalinism. Any unfairness*
> *or rudeness that accrues from the "security*
> *profiling" of Middle Eastern young males is*
> *dwarfed by efforts of Islamic fascists them-*

selves — here in the U.S., in the UK, the Neth-
erlands, France, Turkey, and Israel — to mur-
der Westerners and blow up civilians.

Since a phobia is an unreasonable fear of something, the term is inappropriately applied to Islam.
It is not unreasonable to fear being blown to bits in
the name of Islam. As of today, 25,564 deadly
attacks have been carried out in the name of Islam
since 9/11. They can strike anywhere. They could
be a man, woman, or child. They don't look any
particular way; they could be Chinese or European
or African or Middle Eastern, young or old. But
they are driven by a particular ideology — specifically, the teachings of the religion of Islam. And
that doesn't count, of course, the many plots that
were stopped by competent security forces.

Islamophobia is not a good word for it. A better term might be "legitimate concern."

9. "Isn't this bigotry?"

When you say anything negative about Islamic
doctrine, one of the responses you'll typically get
is an implication that you are a bigot. If you ever
hear this, your first response should be to define
"bigot." Most people don't really know what it
means. They only know it is a bad thing and has
something to do with racism.

A bigot is "strongly partial to his own group, religion, race, or politics and is intolerant of those who differ."

So someone who is a Christian, for example, and is intolerant of anyone who is not a Christian, is a bigot. Or anyone who is Chinese and intolerant of anyone who is not Chinese, is a bigot. If the group to which you are partial is your race, then bigotry is the same as racism.

There are definitely people trying to stop Islam's relentless encroachment who are motivateed by bigotry. But criticism of Islamic doctrine is not bigotry.

You can answer the bigotry objection very simply. First, define it. And then say, "I am partial to groups who want to support the continued existence of the United States (or the UK, or wherever you are). So I guess in that sense, I am a bigot — I am partial to a group and intolerant of subversives. I don't want our government overthrown or subverted by someone who wants to follow Sharia law. I am against any movement trying to take away women's rights, freedom of religion, and freedom of speech, which is what orthodox Muslims are doing."

And maybe you can add something like this: "But if that can be defined as a bigot, I hope you are that kind of bigot, too. Are you?"

The real objection of someone who fears you are a bigot is that you are against everyone if they are not of your religion, your race, or your political persuasion. And that you might be intolerant of such people simply because of those things.

Is it true? Do you believe that your way is the only right way? Are you intolerant of anyone not like you?

Do you believe others have a right to worship as they wish? Do you believe people of other races are entitled to the same human rights as you?

If you are a conservative and you have liberal friends, if you're a Jew and have a Buddhist, Hindu, or Christian friend, if you're Anglo-Saxon but have a Mexican friend, you're probably not a bigot. And if your accuser says so, you can point out these things and then get back to the real issue: The doctrine of Islam, our right to criticize it, and the danger it presents to the free world.

10. "Are you a hatemonger? I don't believe in promoting hatred."

When you criticize Islam, you may very well be accused of being a "hater," as if telling people about basic Islamic doctrines means you advocate hatred toward Muslims as the solution. And nobody likes a hater, or wants to be one.

This objection is fairly easy to answer. Here are three possible ways to respond:

Answer number one: Hatred is not the answer. If anything, I am anti-hatred. That's why I am trying to expose Islamic teachings: Sharia law includes a system of legally-mandated hatred. Muhammad is their model, and he expressed hatred toward non-Muslims. He maligned them, robbed them, tortured them, killed them, raped them, and took them as slaves. And Muslims are supposed to follow his example.

Answer number two: I'm talking about the teachings, not the people. Some Muslims follow the teachings, and some are Muslim in name only. But non-Muslims need to know about the teachings, because many of the most fundamental Islamic teachings are about how to deal with non-Muslims. According to the doctrine, we must be subjugated under Islamic law. All of us. Voluntarily or by force. And the tens of millions or hundreds of millions who follow Islamic doctrine to the letter are actively working toward that end. They have gained control over how Islam is taught in American schoolbooks. Devoted followers have set up organizations in the United States and other Western democracies with the express purpose of undermining those democracies from within. We need to know about this stuff. It is affecting us already.

Answer number three: If I say the teachings of communism advocate ending economic inequalities, does that make me a hatemonger? If I say Republicans advocate smaller government, does that make me a hater? If I say Buddhists believe in reincarnation, does that make me a hater? But if I say the teachings of Islam advocate striving to institute worldwide Sharia law, how does *that* make me a hatemonger? It doesn't make sense. Where did you come up with that?

When you answer these questions, think of the question itself as an earnest request for knowledge, even if the question comes out as an accusation. People don't really know how to understand what you're doing, so they use the only model they can think of to interpret your actions: They think you must be like a racist or a religious bigot or something along those lines.

So a helpful response is to *give them a better model* to interpret you with. What you're doing is educating, not hatemongering. Urge them to read the Koran for themselves to find out more about it.

11. "You should really talk to some Muslims. You're getting all this from books."

This objection seems sensible if you haven't had time to think about it, but it is meaningless — unless, of course, you've just made the blunder of overgeneralizing (saying something like, "All Mus-

lims treat their women badly") — in which case,
you should immediately correct yourself by talking about Islamic *doctrine* rather than talking
about "Muslims."

But assuming you are making no such blund-
ers, here is a possible answer to this objection:
"I *have* talked to Muslims. And I've met some very
nice Muslims. They are either ignoring some of the
basic, mainstream Islamic teachings (and I'm glad
they are) or they are using taqiyya, which is the
Islamic principle of 'religious deception' or deception for the sake of Islam.

"But hopefully, they're simply genuinely nice
people who are ignoring some of the religious
principles of Islam. You see, if a Muslim is truly a
friend to me (a non-Muslim), he or she is violating
the doctrine of Islam: A Muslim is forbidden to
befriend a non-Muslim. I'm not making this up. It's
in the Koran and it's stated very clearly.

"But either way, it doesn't change the fact that
the *doctrine* of Islam is hazardous to non-Muslims
and we should learn about it. Sixty-one percent of
the Koran is about how Muslims are supposed to
deal with non-Muslims. Millions of Muslims in the
world are devout believers in that doctrine.

"What I'm advocating is simple public knowledge. It's amazing how little most people know
about Islam, especially given how much these
teachings are impacting current events. Anyway, I
think you should stop believing what other people
tell you, including me, and just read the Koran

yourself. Get to the bottom of this thing once and for all."

12. "But aren't there *peaceful* passages in the Koran too?"

This one is easy because the Islamic world already has a well-established answer to the question. Every reader of the Koran, since the time it was written, has noticed the conflicting messages. And they've had the question, "When two passages from the Koran conflict, which one should I follow?"

The Koran itself answers the question. It says if two passages conflict, the passage revealed *later* is better than the one revealed *earlier*. The principle is known as *abrogation*. The later passage abrogates (supersedes or overrides) the earlier passage.

Since the order in which the chapters of the Koran were written was carefully recorded, each instance of a conflicting passage is easily settled. The bad news is: The peaceful passages were some of the first written, and the intolerant, violent passages were almost all written later.

So the short answer is, "Yes, there are peaceful passages in the Koran. But they have all been abrogated."

13. "People take what they want from any writings. You can pretty much justify anything if you quote it out of context."

Some day in the near future (if it hasn't happened already), you'll be telling someone what's in the Koran, and they'll respond with something like this: "Well, the Bible has a lot of violent passages too, and people can pretty much read these holy books however they want to read them."

In other words, it's not what is written in those books; the problem is that some people are looking to justify violence and they will pick and choose passages to help their justifications.

The person you're talking with will probably think her or his comment will end your line of reasoning, because for someone who doesn't know much about Islam or the Koran, the comment seems like a legitimate objection.

This is a perfect opportunity to explain a little about the differences between other religious doctrines and Islamic doctrines. Not only is the *content* different, the *way* it was written is different too. So here's one possible way to answer:

> "The Koran is different in several import-
> ant ways from any other religious book. Do
> you know how it was written?"

The person probably doesn't even know that much, and I think it's important to establish — in this subtle and inoffensive way — just how much your listener doesn't know about Islam. It helps to create a frame of mind conducive to listening to new information.

So when the person says, "No, I don't," you can continue: "The entire Koran was written by one man, Muhammad, over the course of his lifetime. It took him 23 years to write it. Actually he didn't *write* it, he recited it because he was illiterate. It isn't full of metaphors or symbolism. It isn't a collection of things written over many centuries by many different authors like some other religious books. It is mostly graphic descriptions of hell and Paradise, and direct instructions on how a Muslim should behave, dictated to Muhammad from Allah (through an angel).

"In other words, you can't really justify anything with it that it doesn't say. You may be able to do that with some other religious books, but the Koran says very clearly and directly what a Muslim must do to avoid hell and make it to Paradise. By the way, do you already know about the principle of abrogation?"

The person you are talking to will probably shake his or her head. So you can explain it: "Well, since the different chapters, or *suras*, came as revelations periodically over Muhammad's lifetime, and since his circumstances changed so much, the nature of the revelations changed too. So there are conflicting passages in the Koran.

This may catch your listener's interest.

"Some passages encourage Muslims to be tolerant toward other religions, and some passages encourage Muslims to be intolerant and even violent to unbelievers.

"But, oddly enough, the Koran *itself* has some passages explaining what to do with its own contradictions," and so on.

14. "There are millions of Muslims in this country and they're not blowing things up."

This objection goes to the core of the issue. The question is, "If it's true what you're saying about Islamic doctrine — if it's true that violence against non-Muslims is mainstream Islam and it is explicit and inherent in the Koran and Hadith and Sira — why aren't *all* Muslims trying to kill us?"

Below are four possible ways to answer this question. All of them are good opportunities to widen your listener's understanding of Islam.

Answer number one: Islam's prime directive is not to kill all non-Muslims. It is to bring all people under the rule of Sharia law. According to mainstream and accepted Islamic doctrine — accepted in all schools of Islamic jurisprudence — once non-

Muslims are subjugated, they are to be given the choice between one of the following: a) converting to Islam, b) living as a subjugated, second-class citizen (a dhimmi, but only if they are Jews or Christians), or c) execution. But that is *after* conquering the non-Muslims by war.

But for many Muslims living in Western democracies, they do not believe we are in a state of open warfare yet. We are in the "pre-conquest" stage.

Muhammad set the example. When he was not powerful — when Muslims were a minority in Mecca — Muhammad did not kill anyone. He focused on gaining converts. It was only when he could act from a position of strength that he began using violence. All Muslims are supposed to follow his example. This one fact alone can fully explain the lack of universal violence among Muslims against non-Muslims.

But of course, many Muslims aren't aware of this program. The imams may be aware of it, but many regular Muslim citizens don't know about Islam's prime directive, and at the moment, they do not need to know, as far as the imams are concerned. It is best for Islam's ultimate goal if they just innocently go about their lives having babies and raising them to be devout Muslims.

Not many Muslims have read the Koran or understand it, partly because it has been made difficult to understand, and sometimes because many Muslims are Muslim in name only (MINOs), or simply Muslim by birth, and they haven't taken the time to learn what they are supposed to do, or if they have, they're not interested in pursuing it. They'd like to just make money, have a family, etc.

Unfortunately, many of these apatheistic Muslims are unwitting sleeper cells.

Many Muslims are *secretly* heterodox (don't follow the teachings strictly). They may be a little vulnerable to recruitment into more orthodox Islamic organizations, but their children are even *more* vulnerable to recruitment, which explains why the study in Britain found that *second* generation British Muslims are more "radical" (more orthodox) than their immigrant parents.

But for the moment, the MINOs are trying to do the one thing a Muslim must never do: Ignore the Messenger (Muhammad). So they may be perfectly nice, peace-loving people. I know three Muslims, and they are some of the nicest people I've ever met. None of them prays five times a day, and not one of them has read the Koran. I know far more about Islam than any of them.

But the point is, they are three of the "millions of Muslims" who are not blowing things up. But notice this says nothing about the *doctrine*. These perfectly nice MINOs can function like sleeper cells without even knowing it. How? By simply raising their children to believe they are Muslims. They may not practice any of the five pillars of Islam, but they *identify* themselves as Muslims (apostasy — leaving Islam — can be difficult, uncomfortable, and even dangerous).

So they go along with the program, and say things like, "the Koran is the final word of Allah" because they're supposed to; it's part of the Muslim identity.

Then as a teen perhaps, their child goes to a mosque to explore his roots a little and meets someone there who *has* read the Koran and believes in it, and he says to the kid, "do you realize your parents are hypocrites?" And what young, rebellious teen is not willing to hear that?

So the recruiter gives him a copy of the Koran and tells him to read it, and talks to him about what it really says (that Muslims are the best people in the world, that he must follow the Koran's teachings or he has no chance of getting to Paradise and a good chance of burning in a fiery torment forever).

Yikes! The kid reads the Koran, something he has always been told is the direct word of Allah, and that's how we end up with "homegrown jihadists" like Nidal Hasan (the Fort Hood shooter), Faisal Shahzad (the Times Square bomber), Umar Abdulmutallab (the underwear bomber), Mujahid Muhammad (the Little Rock killer), Adam Gadahn (the American-born senior al-Qaeda operative), John Walker Lindh (the American fighting on the side of Afghanistan), the London bombers, and on and on and on.

So yes, there are millions of Muslims who are not blowing anything up at the moment. But that does not mean we don't have a problem and we can all forget about it and go on about our business.

Answer number two: Most people have natural empathy for other people. The vast majority (prob-ably close to 98 percent) of human beings, by and large do not like to hurt other people or even animals. It's plain ol' humanity.

So it seems likely that even some Muslims who *know* about Islam's prime directive choose to ignore it and hope they can get away with it.

But even though 98 percent of people have natural human empathy, far more than 2 percent of Muslims believe in the political objectives of Islam and are actively working to achieve them, including through violence.

One of the things violent cultures have always done to override this natural human empathy is to convince their believers that the enemy is not human. Muhammad called Jews, for example, "apes and pigs." Throughout the Koran, non-Muslims are depicted horribly. This *indoctrination*, of course, can override natural human empathy.

But for people who have *not* been educated in a madrassa or who had MINOs for parents and no access to a mosque, and who have not read the Koran, none of that indoctrination took place and their natural human empathy prevents them from being an immediate danger to non-Muslims.

Answer number three: Jihad means "to strive in the way of Allah," and the striving can be done in many ways. Blowing things up is only one of many ways to accomplish Islam's prime directive.

Many mainstream Muslim organizations in Western democracies have decided that tactically — with some countries and in some circumstances — jihad is best waged non-violently, at least until the percentage of Muslims in the population is higher.

It's a *tactical* decision, not a moral one. Jihad and the basic, supremacist nature of Islamic teachings have not been rejected; the violence has been postponed for strategic reasons.

The strategy is to build up the number of followers, increase political power, seek concessions and accommodations to Islam, convince people Islam is benign, and most importantly, disable free speech (to make it a crime to educate non-Muslims about Islam).

This is not a guess. Their purposes and strategies have been uncovered in FBI raids and the undercover infiltration of a key Islamic organization in America (Google "Holy Land Foundation trial" for more information).

Answer number four: Another possible way to respond to this objection is to use the same statement Robert Spencer uses in almost every one of his speeches: "In Islam, as in all other religions, there is a spectrum of belief, knowledge, and fervor."

What it says in the doctrine does not *necessarily* correlate with what any particular individual will do. Enough Muslims are following the doctrine that we can't really ignore it, but that doesn't mean every single person who calls himself a Muslim is doing what the doctrine says he should do.

Okay, now you have four possible ways to respond to this objection. While answering, keep in mind that most people are behind the curve on jihad. They still think what we need to do is "stop the terrorists." That's only part of a much larger and far more sinister threat: The ultimate annihilation of civilizations, as was done very successfully in the first two jihads. Turkey used to be Christian. Now it is 99 percent Muslim. Afghanistan used to be Buddhist. Pakistan used to be Hindu. The entire Middle East and North Africa used to be non-Muslims, of course.

But I don't suggest you tell people about the annihilation of civilizations until you get them up to speed on some more basic information about Islam. If you go too far too fast in the educational process, they will mentally place you in the category of "complete nutcase" and will stop listening. Talk basics first. Let the full implications come later.

15. "My family and my community is Muslim, and none of us are terrorists."

If you hear a Muslim say this, rather than jumping in and crying "taqiyya!" I think the best approach is to take their statement as a sincere and even innocent and legitimate objection, just as a matter of policy.

I once got this objection from a young woman who I knew was promiscuous and partied a lot (including drinking alcohol, which Islamic doctrine says is taboo). My response was, "I am criticizing Islamic *teachings*. You do not follow these teachings, so what are you objecting to?" She never said another word about it. I think she was afraid someone in her family would find out about her lifestyle, and didn't want me saying any more.

But I generally avoid telling Muslims about the doctrines of Islam. If they don't know, I would much rather they remained ignorant, unless I feel I could actually turn them into apostates (someone who leaves the religion). And if they already know the doctrines, I am unlikely to dislodge their belief, so it's a waste of time.

But occasionally you will accidentally have to engage Muslims. For the most part, you can simply say, "I'm glad you and your family and community are not terrorists." But if you have an audience — if this is a public conversation, or if it's a comment on Facebook or a blog or YouTube, and others are waiting to see how you will respond — here's a way you could answer the objection:

Terrorism is a *tactic*. The goal is to bring "the light of Islam" to the world. That is one of a Muslim's primary religious obligations. It is known as jihad. The purpose of jihad is not to blow things up. The purpose is to bring Islamic law to the world; to ultimately create the conditions wherein all people on earth are under the legal rule of Sharia law, which is considered by Muslims as a holy law, a law that brings order and morality into a society.

One way to accomplish this goal is with intimidation. You can frighten people with your willingness to do violence if they don't comply. If you have sufficient power to inflict the violence, this tactic can be very effective. In places like India, where there is a sizable minority of Muslims, the tactic is powerful.

But in a place like the United States, where the Muslim population is only a few percent, it is much less effective. So other tactics are used.

The Muslim Brotherhood — the largest Muslim organization in the world — has set up lots of seemingly mainstream and "moderate" organizations, working legally within the United States and other Western democracies, to accomplish the goal of getting non-Muslims to adhere to the legal standards of Islamic law, one small concession at a time.

For example, it is against Sharia law to criticize Islam or Muhammad, and these organizations are working hard to make American non-Muslims follow this Islamic rule.

So CAIR will sue people, for example, or get the media involved in conflicts so someone gets fired, and they use many other legal means to suppress the free expressions guaranteed under our Constitution but illegal under Sharia, and they often succeed.

One example of their success occurred when Muslims in the Middle East were rioting over the Muhammad cartoons. Only *one* newspaper in the United States reprinted the cartoons. Every other newspaper, in essence, followed Sharia law.

Groups like CAIR and ISNA are funded, in part, by donations from Muslims. And many other politically-oriented Muslim projects are funded by mosques around the country. So if the Muslim who has a family and community who "are not terrorists" but are paying their zakat, they may well be funding this ongoing non-violent jihad without knowing it. If they are a member of any Muslim organizations like the Muslim Students Association or ISNA, they may be advancing the agenda without ever doing anything that might be considered "terrorism."

My general goal when answering an objection is to try to use the objection as an opportunity to get more information into the other person's head. Not to argue. To educate.

Now in this case, you are answering a Muslim, but the purpose is not to educate the Muslim. Try to educate anyone who is listening. I don't recommend arguing with Muslims at any time. You have more important things to do. Focus your attention on educating your fellow non-Muslims. But *if* the situation comes up, and *if* there is a non-Muslim audience, use your conversation with the Muslim to help educate your fellow non-Muslims. Get some important, basic facts into their heads.

16. "Fundamentalism is fundamentalism."

I've heard this one implied and also spoken aloud. In other words, the dangerous thing is the fundamentalism itself, and it is not proper to single out any one religion because they all have their extremists.

The answer to this is, as always, basic education about Islam. Underlying the statement is one big assumption that happens to be wrong — that the core teachings of all religions are roughly the same. When you clear up this misconception, the argument "fundamentalism is fundamentalism" will lose its foundation.

The truth is, not all religions are the same. Islam has several precepts in its core teachings, written in their most holy book, the Koran (which you have hopefully read cover to cover by now) that are different from any other religion.

For example, the Koran and Muhammad's example make it clear it is a Muslim's duty to refuse to be friends with a non-Muslim, to deceive them if it will help the cause of Islam, to strive to subjugate non-Muslims politically, and if they resist, Muslims should make war on the unbelievers and slaughter them. The texts don't *imply* this. Nobody needs to *try* to interpret it that way or read between the lines. The doctrine says it quite clearly.

So a "fundamentalist" who is following Islam will be (and, as you can see around the world, IS) quite a bit more willing to kill people just because they are unbelievers than, say, a fundamentalist Buddhist or Taoist.

Another thing very different about the Koran is that it was communicated in very straightforward prose by one man. Most non-Muslims do not even know that much about Islam. The Koran is not a collection of writings from different sources. It isn't metaphorical. It isn't strewn with allegories open to interpretation.

If you have read the Koran, you may speak with authority about this. The person who says "fundamentalism is fundamentalism" is a (probably well-meaning) non-Muslim who has never read the Koran. Your best approach is to convince them that they are relying on assumptions and hearsay, and cannot know what's true about Islamic doctrine until they, too, read the Koran for themselves.

If some of your friends or family are still reluctant to believe a religion could actually promote hatred or intolerance or violence, ask them some questions. Don't try to get them to answer the questions. Just ask them to think about or wonder about this:

Why do we have so many problems with Muslims but not Buddhists? Why are we constantly urged to tolerate and co-exist with Muslims but not Buddhists? Western culture isn't more similar to Buddhism than Islam. So why doesn't anybody feel the need to convince us to tolerate Buddhists?

Could it be that the tenets of the religions themselves are different?

I like to use Buddhism for comparison because if you are in a Western country and talk about Christianity or Judaism, it doesn't work as an example, because most people consider Western culture to be a "Judeo-Christian" culture. Buddhism is outside the normal biases, so can be used as a good comparison.

A Zen master is a Buddhist *fundamentalist*. Zen masters try to practice Buddhism in its *pure* form. They try to do things the way Buddha did them, and they try to follow Buddha's teachings. They live austere lives devoted to meditation and teaching, just like Buddha did. They try to focus more on direct experience than on learning doctrines (something Buddha repeatedly emphasized in his teachings). They try not to conceptualize their experience too much. Zen masters get their students to learn about their own minds from long periods of meditation (rather than solely from listening to a teacher or reading).

A Buddhist fundamentalist cultivates a state of calmness and kindness, and cultivates the ability to keep her or his attention in the present moment and not in the past, the future, or lost in thought.

These are Buddhist fundamentalists.

If Zen devotees work hard, most of them will achieve a state of abiding inner peace and a profound and lasting feeling of kindness toward almost everyone.

Islamic fundamentalists try to practice Islam in its *pure* form. They try to do things the way Muhammad did them, and they try to follow Muhammad's teachings. They live austere lives devoted to jihad. They don't sit around contemplating their navels. They prove their devotion with *action*. They try to make the law of Allah the supreme law of the world. They devote their lives to fulfilling the political goal of Islam, just as Muhammad dedicated *his* life to it, and just as Muhammad taught his followers to do.

An Islamic fundamentalist cultivates animosity toward non-Muslims and works toward the day when all non-Muslims are either subjugated as dhimmis, converted to Islam, or dead.

These are Islamic fundamentalists.

If Islamic devotees work hard, most of them will find themselves in some form of warfare with non-Muslims and ideally will be killed fighting in the way of Allah.

Are all fundamentalists dangerous? Are all ideologies the same? Would it matter to you what kind of fundamentalist you had as your neighbor? Would it matter to you what kind of fundamentalist your children chose as close friends or heroes? Would it matter to you what kind of fundamentalist your country allowed to immigrate to your country?

17. "Haven't mosques and churches and synagogues been sitting side-by-side in the Middle East for a thousand years?"

The implication is, of course, that if all you're saying about Islam is true, then all Christians and Jews who live in Islamic lands would have been wiped out or converted centuries ago. But they're still there, and not only are they still there, they have their houses of worship still standing there, proving Islam's tolerance, right?

The answer is, "Yes, mosques and churches and synagogues sit side-by-side in the Middle East (except Saudi Arabia)." But the missing piece of information is the dhimma laws. So the rest of the answer is, "Islam allows for Jews and Christians (but not Buddhists, Hindus or atheists) to continue practicing their religions as long *as they keep the contract of the dhimma.*"

Then, of course, you can explain what dhimmitude is and how it works. Dhimmis must pay a tax, usually 25 to 50 percent of their income. Muslims do not pay this tax. It is "protection money," which is not a slander — that's how Islamic texts describe it.

As long as dhimmis pay this money and accept the other stipulations and humiliations required of dhimmis, they are allowed to live. If they break the dhimma contract, their lives are forfeit.

Other stipulations are many. Under Sharia law, dhimmis are not allowed to repair their churches or synagogues, nor are their religious buildings allowed to be taller than the mosques.

Jews and Christians are not allowed to display any symbols of their religion where a Muslim may see them. Dhimmis are not allowed to make any religiously-oriented sounds (like singing a hymn, for example, or praying aloud) where a Muslim might hear it. They are not allowed to talk to a Muslim about their religion. The list goes on and on.

If a dhimmi violates any of these rules, the penalty is death. If they keep these rules, then yes, they can have their churches and synagogues, and so we see them throughout the Middle East and North Africa, since prior to the Muslims conquering what we now know as the Middle East, it was primarily Christians and Jews who populated those lands. Their numbers have dwindled down over the last 1400 years as they fled or were converted or killed, but there are still some remnants of the Christians and Jews left in those areas.

Islamic law covers every aspect of life, and when it is applied, Islam essentially eliminates other cultures until there is nothing left except Islam. The numbers of Jews and Christians in Muslim countries has shrunk to almost nothing and continues to dwindle.

When you are done explaining how and why synagogues and churches can be found in Muslim countries, explain that this is basic Sharia law, and recommend the book, *Sharia Law for Non-Muslims*. This slim volume gives a great overview of this fascinating topic, and can be a real eye-opener for people.

18. "You're taking the verses of the Koran out of context."

I received a comment I've heard many times:

"I have been a Muslim all my life. Westerners in general love to take the verses of the Koran out of their historical context and just blindly accuse Islam and the Koran of violence. For your information, many of the 'violent' verses were revealed to prophet Mohammed (peace be upon him) when he was in a state of war with the pagans of Mecca. So read the reason for a revelation very carefully. Then you will understand what those verses were intended for."

I posted several responses to this, and I thought they might give you some good ideas about how to approach this objection. Here is part of my response:

I'm going to answer you in several ways, not because I believe I will change your mind, but because everyone who comes after you to read these comments may learn something from our interaction.

First of all, I have gotten many comments like yours. In fact, I've gotten so many that I wrote a "standard" answer which you can read here: *Message to Peaceful Muslims* (I left a link to this).

My more specific response to what you're saying is this:

1. According to mainstream Islam since the time of Muhammad, the Koran is the perfect, unalterable, eternal word of Allah.

2. It says in the Koran 91 times a Muslim must follow the example of Muhammad.

3. Muhammad was intolerant and violent toward non-Muslims, repeatedly and consistently, as soon as he gained power. He ordered the assassinations of those who insulted him or Islam. He ordered and personally oversaw the beheading of his political prisoners. He raided and plundered and conquered for the last ten years of his life. This is not history as told by his enemies, but history as told in the Sira and the Hadith, written by devout Muslim believers.

4. There are not many peaceful passages in the Koran, but what few exist have all been abrogated by more intolerant and even violent verses revealed to Muhammad later in his prophetic career.

My next response quotes from an excellent article entitled, *Are Judaism and Christianity as Violent as Islam?* By Raymond Ibrahim, who speaks fluent Arabic:

"[Although] Islam's original enemies were... historical (e.g., Christian Byzantines and Zoroastrian Persians), the Koran rarely singles them out by their proper names. Instead, Muslims were (and are) commanded to fight *the people of the book*— 'until they pay the tribute out of hand and have been humbled' and to 'slay the idolaters wherever you find them.'

"The two Arabic conjunctions 'until' (hata) and 'wherever' (haythu) demonstrate the perpetual and ubiquitous nature of these commandments: There are still 'people of the book' who have yet to be 'utterly humbled' (especially in the Americas, Europe, and Israel) and 'idolaters' to be slain 'wherever' one looks (especially Asia and sub-Saharan Africa). In fact, the salient feature of almost all of the violent commandments in Islamic scriptures is their open-ended and generic nature: 'Fight them [non-Muslims] until there is no persecution and the religion is God's entirely.' Also, in a well-attested tradition that appears in the hadith collections, Muhammad proclaims:

> "I have been commanded to wage war against mankind until they testify that there is no god but God and that Muhammad is the Messenger of God; and that they establish prostration prayer, and pay the alms-tax [i.e., convert to Islam]. If they do so, their blood and property are protected."

And my final response to the objection was this:

Whether *you* believe the Koran commands you to be intolerant or violent towards non-Muslims, many Muslims *do* obviously believe it, and they are using the Koran to justify their violence against non-Muslims all over the world, and they have been doing so for 1400 years.

It has been such a consistent theme, a web site keeps track of all the violence committed in the name of Islam around the world, and has been doing so since 9/11. As of today, September 2nd, 2010, fifteen thousand, nine hundred and sixty-six attacks on non-Muslims have been committed since 9/11 in the name of Islam, and most of these attacks have killed and wounded many people.

Citizen Warrior is a web site devoted to helping non-Muslims understand where this perpetual hostility against them is coming from and figuring out what to do about it. If you'd like to start a web site for Muslims that would convince *them* of what you're trying to convince *me* of, I would applaud your efforts.

But if you're trying to convince me that because *you* don't believe the Koran encourages violence against non-Muslims then none of the rest of the Muslims do either (or that the Koran really doesn't encourage intolerance and violence toward non-Muslims), your task is hopeless. I have read the Koran cover to cover.

19. "But jihad is an internal struggle."

When you mention jihad, many people will say that "jihad means struggle." They say (or imply) that since Islam is a religion of peace, then jihad is the spiritual struggle to perfect oneself, and the terrorists are taking it out of context or twisting and distorting the perfectly peaceful Islamic doctrine into something violent.

This objection is easily dispatched. Bill Warner has done the footwork of counting every mention of jihad in Bukhari's hadith. As Wikipedia says, "Most Muslims view this (Bukhari's) as their most trusted collection of hadith and it is considered the most authentic book after the Koran."

In reading Bukhari's collection of hadith, this is what Warner found:

"The Hadith of Bukhari gives all of the tactical details of jihad. A simple counting method shows that 3% of the hadiths are about the inner struggle, whereas, 97% of the hadiths are about jihad as war. So is jihad the inner struggle? Yes, 3%. Is jihad the war against kafirs (non-Muslims)? Yes, 97%."

That's a great answer. I've used it many times, and it completely answers the objection, removing it from the conversation as an issue.

And it goes beyond answering the objection. It points to a common fundamental misconception many people have about Islamic terrorists: That their interpretation is something only a small extreme or fringe element believes. The truth is, relentless violence against (and subjugation of) non-Muslims is a longstanding element of mainstream Islamic doctrine.

The terrorists have not "hijacked" a religion of peace. This kind of intolerance toward non-Muslims has been a cornerstone of mainstream Islam for 1400 years.

An objection like this is an opportunity. If you study the answers to objections, you should actually look *forward* to objections because they give you great opportunities to educate and awaken another potential ally in this fight.

20. "Criticizing Islam will push the moderates into the arms of the extremists."

In an article entitled, *Taking the Fight to Islam*, Andrew Anthony writes:

> Does [Ayaan Hirsi Ali's] bald delivery not further alienate Muslims, forcing them to cling to traditional values? Hirsi Ali is too smooth of skin and composure to bristle, but it is obviously an accusation she finds irritating...
>
> "Tariq Ramadan is filled with contempt for Muslims because he believes they have no faculties of reason," she replies in a beguilingly friendly tone, as though she had remarked that he had an excellent taste in shirts. "If I say that terrorism is created in the name of Islam suddenly they take up terrorism? He gives me so much more power than I have. Why don't my remarks make *him* turn to terrorism?"

This objection is fairly common — that by educating non-Muslims about Islam, we are risking
the possibility that otherwise peaceful Muslims
will take up arms and join the third jihad. But the
argument doesn't have much heft if you give it
even five minutes of thought.

I heard Robert Spencer put it this way, in essence: Do you really think devout Muslims or even
heterodox Muslims will be swayed by the teachings of a non-Muslim? That's ridiculous.

Spencer was commenting on the new limitat-
ions imposed on U.S. security agencies to avoid
using such terms as "Islamic terrorists" because it
might make "moderate Muslims" want to blow
things up. He asked how anyone could think that a
believing Muslim would use the *U.S. government* as
a reliable source on the teachings of Islam? Good
question.

A Muslim, of course, will be influenced much
more strongly by their own personal (usually life-
long) understanding of Islam, their own reading of
Islamic doctrine, their own imam, the teachings of
their own sect and their parents, etc.

To believe that a non-Muslim pointing out the
supremacist teachings of Islam would cause a Muslim to give up his own understanding of his faith
and become a jihadist seems, to put it mildly, highly unlikely.

Let's look at this another way. By definition, a
"moderate Muslim" must reject some basic Islamic
principles. Of course, for someone who knows

little about Islam, this will not be obvious. But once they learn about Islam, this much will be clear.

Does it make any sense that a "moderate Muslim" who *rejects* some of Islam's teachings would become a fundamentalist because I am educating non-Muslims about those rejected teachings? Will my educational efforts make the moderate Muslim embrace what he has rejected and become an "extremist?"

We got this comment on one of our articles (*Message to Peaceful Muslims*):

> Moderation is the enemy of any extremist. They thrive in a black-and-white world. This post agrees with the vision of extremistic Muslims: either you're a Muslim or you're a non-Muslim. This post states that a good Muslim is not relevant, because it does not fit in this black-and-white world.
>
> Not a good Muslim, but Citizen Warrior is helping extremist Islam to grow.
>
> Saying that not the extremists but Islam itself is the problem, you are creating a Western version of jihad. "So you Muslims want jihad? Fine, we can do that as well! I will declare myself a warrior."
>
> Good luck with it.

This was my response:

To think that what a non-Muslim says about Islam will change a believing Muslim's worldview is absurd.

Imagine Amhed, a peace-loving "Muslim in name only" (MINO) who thinks Islam means peace. He's a nice guy. He's never read the Koran, but his parents were Muslims, so he considers himself a Muslim.

And then he reads some non-Muslim blogger saying "true" Muslims are intolerant toward non-Muslims. Will Ahmed become intolerant toward non-Muslims now?

Don't hold your breath. I know enough MINOs to know they are not influenced by anything I say. They think I just don't understand. And devout Muslims would be even *less* influenced by a non-Muslim blogger.

If you are a Christian, would you be influenced by a Muslim telling you what Christians believe? Or telling you what it says in the Bible? Or how to be a good Christian?

What your criticism says is that what I write will influence Muslims who are against violence to *become* violent.

Not only do I have almost no impact on Muslim beliefs because I am a non-Muslim, but my audience is almost entirely non-Muslims. My job here is to alert the hundreds of millions of non-Muslims living in free countries to the basic and often surprising teachings of mainstream Islam. These teachings are being actively hidden by Orthodox Muslims who have actually read the Koran because their political plan works best when non-Muslims don't have a clue.

So what you're asking me to do is to be silent on the slim chance that something I say will influence a Muslim to become intolerant, while at the same time leaving all the non-Muslims I might have reached in the dark.

Hmmm. Let me see...

Nah. I don't think so.

Upon discovering the intolerance and violence that their doctrine really teaches, it seems to me most good-hearted, peace-loving Muslims would be more likely to *leave* their faith than to become more devout. And even if some did become more devout because of something I said, the free world would still be better off if Islam's prime directive was widely known.

Right now, because of widespread non-Muslim ignorance of Islam, the initiatives of politically active Muslim organizations are proceeding almost completely unhindered.

Orthodox Muslims, following the plan set forth by the Muslim Brotherhood (the largest international Muslim organization in the world), have successfully infiltrated and influenced Hollywood, newspapers, television news, textbooks, national security agencies, presidents and even comedians (in the comment I leave a link to an article about each one of these).

How can they get away with this? Because so few non-Muslims know anything about Islam. And what many non-Muslims "know" about Islam is mistaken because all those avenues of public education (listed above) have already been compromised.

I propose to you that this argument was originally created by politically active Muslims in order to silence non-Muslims who are trying to educate other non-Muslims about Islam. This argument was then disseminated widely and taken up by devout multiculturalists because it served their own agenda, and it has now become widespread.

But however it happened, the argument is pathetic. Knowing what it really says in Islamic doctrines clearly has better long-term prospects than pretending it doesn't say those things and silencing anyone who tries to educate non-Muslims about it.

21. "You're cherry-picking verses out of the Koran."

I've never actually heard anyone say this in a conversation, but I've read it many times. The objecttion is a great opportunity to give some good information about Islam. Here is how I would answer it:

The Koran is considered by Muslims as Islam's most holy book. Sixty-one percent of the Koran is about non-Muslims. Islamic writings about what *Muslims* should do is religious. Writings about what non-Muslims should do or how Muslims should deal with non-Muslims is *political*. Therefore, based on Islam's most holy book, Islam is more political (61%) than religious (39%).

There are 245 verses in the Koran that could be considered "positive verses" about non-Muslims. Every single one of those verses have been abrogated by later, negative verses about non-Muslims. Not one positive verse about non-Muslims is left.

In contrast, there are 527 verses of intolerance toward non-Muslims, and 109 verses specifically advocating violence towards non-Muslims. Not one of these verses has been abrogated.

Even if you completely ignore the Koran and only look at what Muslims actually do in the Muslim world, the conclusion is the same. Whenever Muslims get a large enough minority to seize the reigns of power and impose their will, they treat non-Muslims horribly, and eventually drive out non-Muslims or subjugate them, or set up conditions that cause non-Muslims to convert to Islam just to relieve the burden of dhimmitude.

The end result is 57 countries in the world that consider themselves Islamic (member states of the OIC, the largest voting block in the U.N.) and that have perpetually dwindling percentages of non-

Muslims in their countries because their non-Muslims citizens flee, are killed, or convert to relieve the dhimmi burden.

So if I am "cherry-picking" verses out of the Koran, apparently Muslims around the world today, and Muslims throughout Islamic history, have cherry-picked in exactly the same way. What an amazing coincidence!

The fact is, every Muslim is commanded by Allah to follow the example of Muhammad, an example that was written down in great detail. The hadith is an enormous written record of what Muhammad said and did. There are two versions of the hadith, which are very similar, that are considered to be the most authentic by Islamic scholars and the Muslim world throughout its history, one by Sahih Bukhari and the other by Sahih Muslim.

If you count up all references to jihad in Bukhari's voluminous record of Muhammad's life, 97 percent of the passages refer to jihad as bloodshed and warfare against non-Muslims. Three percent of the references are about jihad as an inner struggle. So even if Muslims ignore the Koran completely and simply follow Muhammad's example, they would *still* be violent, aggressive, and intolerant, following the same course as would be described by "cherry-picking verses" out of the Koran.

22. "Wouldn't it be better to support *peaceful* Muslims (than to criticize the *violent* ones)?"

Even if the number of Muslims who believe in the basic political objective of Islam and are willing to vote in that direction (and take other actions) are as small a minority as people hope they are — this small minority is, by definition, more politically active and more committed than the "peaceful majority of Muslims."

If the majority is largely silent and politically-inactive, then it doesn't really matter what they think. They are having little influence in the public sphere.

In other words, the idea of stopping the Islamization of the West by strengthening, encouraging, and supporting politically-apathetic Muslims is a fool's errand. That approach will accomplish little. It will not stop the politically-active Muslims, and it will have very little impact on the apathetic Muslims, since they don't really care much about politics or religion anyway, and they just want to live a normal life in peace.

As a matter of fact, supporting politically-apathetic Muslims may even *strengthen* the recruiting efforts of the jihadists because they will correctly see it as "attacking Islam," since Islam strictly forbids apathy and commands active political participation from every Muslim.

It seems very encouraging when people say, "The vast majority of Muslims are not fanatics about their religion's political goals." But I think the author of *Why the Peaceful Majority is Irrelevant* (which you will read shortly) made a persuasive point when he wrote that totalitarian ideologies do not need a majority to take over, and they never have. A small number of committed fanatics can easily dominate a larger number of people who just want to go about their lives in peace.

So let's try to answer this question: Which approach would work better? Option number one: Educating non-Muslims about Islam's prime directive so enough of us have enough knowledge to vote for policies that will stop the Islamization of the West? Or, option number two: Focus on supporting the peaceful Muslims.

How would we even "support peaceful Muslims," anyway? Give them more of a voice in newspapers, radio, and on television? That may actually make our situation worse, because very few peaceful Muslims are publicly honest (or they are ignorant) about Islam's doctrine. So if they spoke their minds more freely in the media, even *more* people would think Islam really is peaceful and loving, and they'd be even more likely to be fooled by the politically active orthodox Muslims, and thus more likely to continue to yield to Islam's relentless encroachment, giving away concessions to these "peace-loving" people.

No, supporting the peaceful Muslims will not solve the problem. The answer is to educate non-Muslims about Islam, so they know what's going on, so they stop being duped and deluded, and so they will help stop orthodox Islam's slow dismantling of our freedoms.

23. "What about the good verses in the Koran?"

You've probably heard someone quote "good" verses from the Koran. Bill Warner wanted to know exactly how many verses in the Koran are positive for non-Muslims, so he counted them. As you already know, the answer is 245. That's pretty good. That adds up to 4,018 words in the Koran, and comprises 2.6 percent of the total Koranic text.

But, says Warner, "in every case, the verse is followed by another verse that contradicts the 'good' verses." Furthermore, except for seven verses, every "good verse" is abrogated later in the same chapter (known as a "sura"). Those seven exceptions are abrogated in later chapters.

In other words, every single one of the verses in the Koran with a positive message for non-Muslims is abrogated, leaving nothing positive for non-Muslims. Not one verse.

There's more. Warner says, "The media emphasizes Islam's positive verses about the People of the Book, the Jews and Christians. Even this turns out to be illusory. Christians and Jews receive the goodness of Islam only if they agree that their sacred texts are corrupt, the Koran is true, and that Muhammad is a prophet of the Christian and Jewish religion." If they do that, they will get the blessings of Islam. Of course, if they do that, they are no longer Christians or Jews; they're Muslims.

So there is nothing positive in the Koran for non-Muslims. Period. And there are 527 verses in the Koran that are intolerant to non-Muslims, 109 of these verses call on Muslims to make war on non-Muslims. You should memorize these numbers so you can spout them without hesitation in a conversation.

When non-Muslims read the Koran and don't like it, sometimes they're accused of "having an unfavorable view of Islam" or being an Islamophobe. Or they may be simply accused of "hatred."

But, really, what is there to *like* about any of this if you're a non-Muslim?

24. "You are a xenophobe."

The following was posted by Roland Shirk on Jihad Watch, and I thought it might be a useful response against blind multiculturalists:

One of the silliest yet most persistent tactics that I've heard used to dismiss the arguments of civilizational patriots (or anti-jihadists or Islamo-realists — take your pick) is to lump us in with some ideology or another — preferably one that is widely discredited. Some assume that all of us are radically anti-religious, or white supremacist, or thoughtless Colonel Blimps who blindly despise every culture but our own. We believe, in the words of Nancy Mitford's fictionalized father, that "abroad is bloody, and foreigners are fiends." These charges are persistent, and we have to waste a fair amount of time refuting them.

One useful tactic, I suggest, is to turn them on their head. If someone accuses you of being a xenophobe, inquire what the opposite of that is. Most likely, your critic will say something like: "A tolerant person," or "a liberal." At that point, you can correct him: "No, the counterpart of someone who is mindlessly hostile to foreign people and things is someone who promiscuously accepts them, who snobbishly prefers them over things home-grown and domestic. If you think I'm a xenophobe, I suggest you might unwittingly have become a xenomaniac. Now what would be a moderate common ground, a

golden mean between those two ex-
tremes?"

25. "The majority of Muslims are peace-loving people."

The following is an article written by Paul Marek
on his blog, *Celestial Junk*. The reason I'm
reprinting this is because one of the most common
responses we get when we mention anything negative about Islamic doctrine is, "But the majority
of Muslims are peace-loving people." This seems
like such a final, decisive, irrefutable, self-evident
conclusion, it makes all your ranting about Islamic
doctrine completely pointless. Or so it seems to
the person who says it.

But from now on, when someone responds to
your educational efforts with "but most Muslims
are peace-loving," school them with Paul's answer.
Here it is:

> I used to know a man whose family were
> German aristocracy prior to World War
> Two. They owned a number of large indus-
> tries and estates. I asked him how many
> German people were true Nazis, and the
> answer he gave has stuck with me and
> guided my attitude toward fanaticism ever
> since.

"Very few people were true Nazis" he said, "but, many enjoyed the return of German pride, and many more were too busy to care. I was one of those who just thought the Nazis were a bunch of fools. So, the majority just sat back and let it all happen. Then, before we knew it, they owned us, and we had lost control, and the end of the world had come. My family lost everything. I ended up in a concentration camp and the Allies destroyed my factories."

We are told again and again by "experts" and "talking heads" that Islam is the religion of peace, and that the vast majority of Muslims just want to live in peace. Although this unquantified assertion may be true, it is entirely irrelevant. It is meaningless fluff, meant to make us feel better, and meant to somehow diminish the specter of fanatics rampaging across the globe in the name of Islam. The fact is, that the fanatics rule Islam at this moment in history. It is the fanatics who march. It is the fanatics who wage any one of 50 shooting wars worldwide. It is the fanatics who systematically slaughter Christian or tribal groups throughout Africa and are gradually taking over the entire continent in an Islamic wave. It is the fanatics who bomb, behead, murder, or honor kill. It is the fanatics who take over mosque after mosque. It is the fanatics who zealously spread the stoning and hanging of rape victims and homosexuals. The hard quantifiable fact is that the "peaceful majority" is the "silent majority" and it is cowed and extraneous.

Communist Russia was comprised of Russians who just wanted to live in peace, yet the Russian Communists were responsible for the murder of about 20 million people. The peaceful majority were irrelevant. China's huge population was peaceful as well, but Chinese Communists managed to kill a staggering 70 million people. The average Japanese individual prior to World War Two was not a war mongering sadist. Yet, Japan murdered and slaughtered its way across South East Asia in an orgy of killing that included the systematic killing of 12 million Chinese civilians; most killed by sword, shovel, and bayonet. And, who can forget Rwanda, which collapsed into butchery. Could it not be said that the majority of Rwandans were "peace loving?"

History lessons are often incredibly simple and blunt, yet for all our powers of reason we often miss the most basic and uncomplicated of points. Peace-loving Muslims have been made irrelevant by the fanatics. Peace-loving Muslims have been made irrelevant by their silence. Peace-loving Muslims will become our enemy if they don't speak up, because like my friend from Germany, they will awake one day and find that the fanatics own them, and the end of their world will have begun. Peace-loving Germans, Japanese, Chinese, Russians, Rwandans, Bosnians, Afghans, Iraqis, Palestinians, Somalis, Nigerians, Algerians, and many others, have died because the peaceful majority did not speak up until it was too late. As for us who watch it all unfold, we must pay attention to the only group that counts; the fanatics who threaten our way of life.

26. "Who are we to tell Muslims to change their beliefs?"

Someone wrote me a long email message, and I wanted to answer it here, because it brought up points worth thinking about. Here is what I wrote:

I've been blogging on Citizen Warrior for eleven years now, and I have never gotten a message like yours. I'm not going to answer all of it, but there were a few things I wanted to answer. The first was your statement, "As an outsider, who am I to tell a foreign cultural group to 'change' their ways or to lobotomize their belief system to make it safer for me?"

You have a right to survive. If someone or something is threatening your survival or even threatening your ability to *thrive*, you have an inborn right to defend your life, whether that right is sanctioned by law or not.

And beyond that, if someone wants to move to a country, that country has every right to say, "We will not allow anyone to immigrate who is intent upon overthrowing our government or causing harm to our citizens." A legitimate government has an obligation to protect its citizens.

If you are my next door neighbor and you have some belief that endangers me, I will insist you change your ways. For example, if you believe that burning plastic bags in your front yard protects you from evil spirits, I will insist you stop it because those fumes are poisonous to me.

I believe people should be able to believe what they want, and do what they want based on those beliefs as long as it doesn't harm others who do not believe that way. If you are doing something that isn't safe for me, that is more important than my respect for your cultural values.

In your email, you also said that trying to make someone change their belief system to make it safer for me is "just as arrogant or non-consensual as Muslim extremists attacking non-Muslims or ex-Muslims." You're basically saying that if I insist that a Muslim change his belief that he should make war on non-Muslims, it is just as arrogant and non-consensual as that Muslim killing me because of his belief. Those are not the same. Not even close.

Later in your email, you said you could only see three possible options for non-Muslims:

1. Become a Muslim. Join the dominant culture, much like Native Americans did when they saw the Great Melting Pot could not be defeated.

2. Fight against Islam. (And because the name of this site is Citizen Warrior, you assume this is the one I choose.)

3. Relocate to a new area.

I would suggest a fourth alternative: Educate non-Muslims. The Native Americans were outgunned and outnumbered. Non-Muslims are not. The biggest problem we have is not Islamic beliefs; it is non-Muslim ignorance. This is *Citizen* Warrior. The military and security agencies have a job to do. But what can citizens do?

Citizens can solve the problem of the vast, inexcusable ignorance of their fellow non-Muslims.

Islam has been gaining ground — not because they are stronger or have a better military or have more intelligent people or have a numerical superiority. They have been gaining ground because *we have been giving it to them.* Why? Because of our ignorance of Islamic doctrine, our ignorance of Islam's prime directive, and our ignorance of Islamic history.

Because we have an already-existing and perfectly understandable commitment to multiculturalism, that commitment is ruling the day for the lack of anything to oppose it or refine it. But if more of us simply knew about Islam, the problem would be largely solved.

As orthodox Muslims pushed for concessions, they would find their way blocked by people who knew better, in the same way a "mark" no longer falls for a con job once they have been educated about it.

If you had never heard of email scams, you might fall for it. But once you know about it, the problem is solved. You simply delete the message, and the harmful intentions on the other end of the line are blocked. If enough people know, the scammers go out of business. It is no longer profitable. It has become a waste of time.

That's what we're trying to accomplish on Citizen Warrior. We aim to put orthodox Muslims out of business.

Final Note:

I have an all-purpose response to any objection you get. Simply ask: "How did you learn about Islam?" Your question will probably reveal to both of you how little the other knows about Islam, and that is always a good place to start.

BEYOND PERSUASION

FOR THE MOST PART, debating is frustrating. If your objective is to change your opponent's mind, debating is a largely useless and futile exercise. If you're debating in public, that's a different story because you can change the *audiences*' minds if you debate well. But when you're speaking one-on-one, debate is a feeble and inadequate weapon in the war of ideas.

You know people who believe Islam is a religion of peace and that you are an Islamophobic bigot for thinking otherwise, and you would like to change their minds. If you try to do it with debate — if you try to do it only by answering arguments with arguments — no matter how good you are at arguing, no matter how many facts you have in your favor, no matter how articulately you express yourself, the odds are a hundred to one against you succeeding.

I'm sure you've already discovered the painful and frustrating truth of this. Back and forth, right and wrong, does not work. You cannot penetrate. Read the book, *The Righteous Mind*, to find out why.

To have any real impact, you need more formidable weapons at your command. What am I talking about? I mean ways of gaining influence and leverage you can *add* to the process of communication, such as dealing with presuppositions (the assumptions your listener started with), or working on small, incremental changes over time, or using Cialdini's principles of influence (which I'll explain shortly), or using NLP rapport techniques (also something I'll explain), or becoming more charismatic.

What we need is *transformational* dialog, not mere debate. We need *influence*, not mere argument. We need to effectively *persuade*, not just get peoples' hackles up and let them dig themselves deeper into their already-justified position.

The following is a list of ideas you can use — ideas you can add to your attempts to educate people about Islam. You already have "argument" in your arsenal. Below are additional tools you can use:

1. Focus on the Undecided

W. Clement Stone, in his book, *The Success System That Never Fails*, said when he first started as a salesman he was spending an inordinate amount of time arguing with people who ended up not buying anything. He expended time and energy on these people with no results. It physically and emotionally wore him out.

So he instituted a rule for himself that if he wasn't getting anywhere after a predetermined amount of time, he would just pleasantly cut the conversation short and go onto his next prospect. He would cut his losses and move on, even if he still hoped he might yet change the person's mind.

His new policy created *startling* results. "Wonderful things happened," he wrote. "I increased my average number of sales per day tremendously."

I think we need to be more efficient in that way too.

In a Citizen Warrior article, I once wrote about a debate conducted by *Intelligence Squared*. Before the debate started, they took a poll of the audience. A certain percentage of them were for the proposition that Islam is a religion of peace, and a certain percentage were against the proposition, and a certain percentage were undecided.

After the debate those who were *for* and those who were *against* hadn't changed their opinions very much, but a lot of the undecideds changed their opinion to "Islam is *not* a religion of peace."

These results indicate that we might benefit from using W. Clement Stone's philosophy and cut our losses when we run across someone whose mind is made up already (unless you have nothing else to do because you're stuck in a waiting room with them for awhile, or unless you have no other people to talk to and you've already convinced everybody you know except those whose minds are already made up).

In other words, let's first focus our efforts on the people in our lives who haven't yet made up their minds about Islam. We will make far more progress in far less time.

Once all of the undecideds have been educated, *then* let's turn our attention to the stubborn ones (approaching the least stubborn first). Let's be efficient. Let's be effective. Let us try to awaken the most people in the shortest possible time.

Another added bonus we might get from this policy is that the stubborn ones may become less so.

Stone says when he began limiting the amount of time he wasted arguing with people, his daily average sales went up. "What's more," he wrote, "the prospect in several instances thought I was going to argue, but when I left him so pleasantly, he would come next door to where I was selling and say, 'You can't do that to me. Every other insurance man would hang on. You come back and write it.' Instead of being tired out after an attempted sale, I experienced enthusiasm and energy for my presentation to the next prospect."

It's possible that the tremendous stubbornness we sometimes run into may ease up when we stop pushing so hard. Doing something unexpected can often cause a change in mental and emotional patterns.

Pleasantly ending an argument without winning may be just the sort of surprising maneuver that could help open someone's mind.

But in the meantime, you'll be focusing your attention on where you can have the most impact.

2. Use Your Body to Help You Reach People

So you want to educate your fellow non-Muslims about Islamic doctrine. Excellent. Bravo. And sometimes you have a difficult time getting the message across. They seem to turn against you. They want to reject your message. You lose rapport. It can sometimes be upsetting.

People who also need to gain rapport so they can influence others — therapists — have discovered many clever ways to gain rapport and prevent losing it.

One of those ways is to *use your body*.

I want you to try an experiment today and tomorrow. You'll be talking with people in the next two days. Every time you're talking to someone, notice how they position their body, and make your body's position similar to theirs.

You don't have to match it perfectly, although they probably wouldn't notice if you did. But if the person's head is tilted slightly, tilt yours slightly. If the person has all his weight on one leg and the other one slightly bent, do the same.

Notice how he has positioned his arms and hands. Make yours somewhat similar. Notice his posture. Make yours similar.

This is one of many ways to gain and keep rapport with someone. You'll find people respond to you better. They will feel closer to you without knowing why. And oddly enough, *you* will feel closer to *them*.

Over the next couple of days, concentrate on this. If you keep it up, it will begin to come naturally. At that point, you will have increased your ability to influence people. Rapport with someone makes them more open to your influence.

If we want to reach people, if we want them to listen to us, if we want our message to penetrate, gaining rapport is a skill worth learning. And using your body is a good place to start.

3. How to Improve Your Persuasive Power By Speaking Their Language

Your mission, should you decide to accept it, is to pay attention today to the words people use to describe their experience. Find out what "representational system" they use the most. Once you learn how to do this, you can start talking to people in a way that will reach them better, because you'll be using the representational system they favor. But for now, your mission is to simply *identify* the primary representational system of everyone you talk to today.

Now that I've given you the mission, I'm going to explain it. A "representational system" is one of three things: Visual, auditory, or kinesthetic.

When you think or remember, you are *representing* reality in your mind.

For example, you can remember what happened yesterday by seeing mental pictures. That would be using your *visual* representational system.

Or you could remember what happened yesterday by recalling what someone told you or the sounds you heard yesterday. That would be using your *auditory* representational system.

Or you could remember how you *felt* yesterday. That's using your *kinesthetic* representational system.

This may seem complicated, but it's not. We have three primary ways to focus our attention and recall memories: Visual, auditory, and kinesthetic. Many of our memories or imaginings include all three representational systems, of course. In other words, you remember what you saw, what you heard, *and* what you felt.

But all of us tend to "favor" one representtational system over the others, in the same way that you favor your right hand or left hand. You tend to use one representational system more than others. You tend to store your most important information in *that* representational system.

You tend to respect and respond to information presented in *that* representational system more than you would if it was presented using a different representational system.

In other words, if you are visually-oriented, and I speak to you using visual terms, what I say will have more impact, will be more persuasive, will be more memorable to you than if I spoke to you using auditory terms.

Speaking in visual terms would be saying things like, "When you read the Koran, you will *see* things in a whole new *light*. You'll get the big *picture*."

Speaking in auditory terms would be saying things like, "When you read the Koran, you are *hearing* the words of Muhammad the way Muslims around the world hear them. It may *sound* like what I'm *saying* does not make sense, but once you read the Koran, it will *click* for you."

Speaking in kinesthetic terms would be saying things like, "When you read the Koran you'll *grasp* the overall negative, hostile *feeling* of Muhammad and Allah toward non-Muslims."

But before attempting to speak someone's language, you must first know what it is. How can you know? *By listening to the way people describe things when they talk.*

That's your assignment today. And ideally, you would keep it up every day until you can easily identify what representational system any person favors. Once you can do that, speaking someone's language is easy.

This exercise will increase your observational powers. And it will increase your ability to connect to people and influence them.

You can practice all day long. Anytime you are speaking with someone, pay attention to which particular kinds of words they use.

This is not as hard as you would think. If I told you to determine whether someone was right or left handed, you would be able to tell just by watching, don't you think? If you observed the person's behavior for awhile, you'd easily identify which hand they favor. You may have known the person for awhile and didn't know if they were right or left handed, but once you pay attention, *once you're looking for it*, you can find out just by paying attention.

You can do the same to discover the representational system they favor. It is only a matter of paying attention.

We need to reach people. We need to help *them* understand what *we* understand about Islam. We need to get past their barriers to listening. So we need to become very good at gaining rapport with people.

One excellent way to improve our rapport and help people to listen to (and respect) what we say is to speak their language — to use the representational system they favor most when we speak.

4. Aim For a Target in Your Conversations

You are more persuasive when you have a goal. Aiming at a *particular* target increases your ability to persuade. The question is, what's a good thing to aim for? My suggestion is to aim at something small that will help educate the person. Ideally something that doesn't cost anything.

If you live in America I think your best bet is to aim for getting the person to subscribe to *ACT! for America's* email updates. The updates don't overwhelm subscribers with too much information and they choose good things to cover. And it's free. It's a small commitment and over time a subscriber will learn more about Islamic doctrine and how those texts are being manifested by orthodox Muslims. Subscribers will also get opportunities to take small actions that will help reinforce their commitment to protecting our freedoms.

I also suggest you set a target for how many people you will get to subscribe. Sales organizations often have contests, which can turn the persuasion process into a game.

Why do they do this? It helps keep the task interesting and fun. And people tend to accomplish more when they have a target they are trying to reach.

Set a target for next month: Decide to get ten people or twenty people, or whatever seems possible for you, to sign up for *ACT! for America's* email updates, and *keep track*. Have a chart on your wall.

And when you get another person to sign up, make another hash mark. Reward yourself at the end of the month if you hit your target.

When you have a target, when there's something you're aiming for, it influences what you say and how you say it — influences it in a positive way. You'll automatically and quite naturally focus more on persuading and connecting than on arguing or "winning" or defeating the other person. Your orientation will be different. Different in a good way. You'll be more effective.

So choose a target. Get the person to subscribe to *Jihad Watch*, for example, or *Europe News*. Or convince them to subscribe to *Inquiry into Islam* (inquiryintoislam.com, one of our sites).

Or get them to "like" your favorite counterjihad Facebook page. Or whatever. Pick something that won't be overwhelming, something easy for them to do, but that will be informative.

If you have created your own counterjihad page on Facebook (and I sincerely hope you have), it would make your successes easy to keep track of. Facebook automatically emails you a weekly report telling you exactly how many fans you gained that week.

However you do it, get people to subscribe to something. It can help the person become more committed to the cause over time. Aim for only a small commitment at first. Let a greater commitment blossom from there.

The principal here is to have a target, and keep your target in mind. Keep aiming for your target. Remember your target while you're talking to people, and always aim for that target in your conversations. This will improve your ability to persuade, it will help you keep a good attitude, and will ultimately lead to more awakened people.

5. Why Girls Are the Key

Below is some information from an article in the *New York Times* called "The Women's Crusade," by Sheryl WuDunn and her husband, Nicholas D. Kristof, the authors of *Half the Sky* and the creators of the *Girl Effect*.

If you help *women*, you help solve many of the problems we have on earth, including the problem of orthodox Islam's expansion.

The reason I feel this should be shared is because about half the non-Muslims who write to me and who want to do something about Islam are not very adept at influencing people. They have a strong desire to share what they know, but they are finding that the *only* people willing to listen are those who already know it and agree with it.

But we need to reach the rest of them. That is a central pivot point for this cause. If enough people knew, we could change national polices. But some people really do not want to know about it, for whatever reason, so the word is not spreading as quickly as it should.

One way to deal with this is to improve your ability to influence people, which I highly recommend. But another way is to choose something that has less built-in ready-made resistance to it. The *Girl Effect* is an excellent candidate.

You can get people to watch and share the videos on the *Girl Effect* website (girleffect.org) and you can convince them to get involved.

You can share with them the information below, and invite them to join the *Girl Effect* on Facebook to get updates.

You can read the book, *Half the Sky: Turning Oppression into Opportunity for Women Worldwide* and share the book with your friends. And for all these things, you will get very little resistance, and yet you will be striking a blow against the advance of orthodox Islam.

In the *New York Times* article, the authors point out that many different significant organizations have come to the same conclusion: That if you want to do something about "extremism" and global poverty, you get the most bang for the buck if you focus on girls and women. "That's why foreign aid is increasingly directed to women," they write. "The world is awakening to a powerful truth: Women and girls aren't the problem; they're the solution..."

When women aren't allowed to get an education, they don't have much impact on the economy. They don't earn money to contribute to their families. But it's worse than that. As the authors put it, "the poorest families in the world spend approximately 10 times as much (20 percent of their incomes on average) on a combination of alcohol, prostitution, candy, sugary drinks and lavish feasts as they do on educating their children (2 percent)."

Now, of course, you can probably guess that it is not the women who are spending the family's meager wealth on beer and prostitutes. It is the men.

Several studies have shown that when women have money, it is more likely to be spent on food and medicine, so the children are healthier. In very poor farmers, sometimes both the men and women grow crops. Some years are good, and when men get extra cash, they tend to spend more on alcohol and tobacco. Women tend to spend surplus income on food. Again, this makes the children healthier.

And this is perhaps the most important thing the authors discovered: "greater female involvement in society and the economy appears to undermine extremism and terrorism. It has long been known that a risk factor for turbulence and violence is the share of a country's population made up of young people. Now it is emerging that male domination of society is also a risk factor."

Apparently these findings have motivated Joint Chiefs of Staff and security specialists to try to figure out how to make sure girls get educated in Afghanistan and other Muslim countries. The long term effect is a weakening of Islamic fundamentalism because Islamic fundamentalism and women's rights cannot coexist. When one rises, the other falls.

6. Conversation Pieces

When you are sharing what you know about Islam's relentless encroachment on the free world, it often helps to have something intensely compelling to share. Below are two items to use in your campaign to influence your friends and family.

The first is entitled "Terrorism That's Personal." It is a set of twelve professional photographs of Muslim women who have been horribly scarred by acid thrown in their faces. The damage done to these women is terrible to see. Shocking.

When Nicholas Kristof, one of the creators of the *Girl Effect*, traveled to Pakistan, he wrote: "I've been investigating such acid attacks, which are commonly used to terrorize and subjugate women and girls in a swath of Asia from Afghanistan through Cambodia (men are almost never attacked with acid). Because women usually don't matter in this part of the world, their attackers are rarely prosecuted and acid sales are usually not controlled. It's a kind of terrorism that becomes accepted as part of the background noise in the region."

If you have the stomach for it, view the pictures. Just Google "Terrorism That's Personal." And share the pictures with people you know. But when you do, make sure you give them some practical actions they can take to do something about it. Whenever you horrify someone, give them something they can *do* about it. It is unkind to do otherwise.

If those images don't motivate someone to want to stop the atrocities, I don't know what will. I also recommend you read and share Nicholas Kristof's original article: *Terrorism That's Personal.*

The second item I want to share with you is from one of my favorite columnists, Phyllis Chesler. In a recent article, she wrote:

> The other day, a twenty-year-old woman was sold at an open auction in Badani Bhutto, Pakistan. Her brothers divided up the money. No one condemned this shameless and abominable act.
>
> It is an act that haunts me.
>
> For a long time now, similar kinds of people (yes, mainly Muslims) have invaded — no, immigrated to — Europe, where they have continued to engage in polygamy, arranged child marriage, forced veiling of women, honor-related violence, including honor murders (17,000 honor-related crimes of violence have been estimated to occur annually in the UK alone), and fe-

male genital mutilation. According to my
new (and about to be published) study,
honor murders in Europe are especially
savage — even more so than in developing
Muslim countries.

You can read the rest of her article online. It's entitled: *Battling Against the Islamification of the World.*

These two shareable items demonstrate the
need to give women and girls human rights in Islamic countries. The situation is urgent, and anyone with normal human feelings will immediately
know something needs to be done.

If you're talking to a friend who doesn't want
to hear about Islam, simply direct them to the *Girl
Effect* or share with them the book, *Half the Sky:
Turning Oppression into Opportunity for Women Worldwide.*

Your friend's efforts to empower women and
protect girls will help curb orthodox Islam's
ultimate goal, and it will be effective even if your
friend never learns a thing about Islamic doctrine.

But one side-effect is that in their efforts to
promote women's rights, they'll come face to face
with the biggest worldwide barrier to women's
rights: Islam's sacred texts. So they might learn
something about orthodox Islam anyway. But it'll
come to them by their own efforts and will therefore have more of an impact on them.

7. People Don't Always Think Like You

You try to share what you have learned about the core teachings of Islam with your fellow citizens, and you have probably met a level of resistance that seems perplexing.

Seth Godin, author of many books on marketing, including *Unleashing the Ideavirus*, said in a recent blog post:

> When you're trying to sell your idea, it's natural to assume that the people you're selling to think the way you do. If you can only show them the facts and stories that led you to believe what you believe, then of course they'll end up where you are... believing.
>
> The problem, of course, is that people don't always think like you.
>
> Go watch some videos of people of different political ideologies talking about why they support a candidate other than your candidate. These people are stupid! They can't conjugate an idea, they have no factual basis for their beliefs, they are clueless, they are ideologues, they are parroting a talking head who knows even less than they do! (And those epithets apply to anyone you disagree with, of course). In fact, they're saying the same thing about you.

Same goes for diehard fans of the other brand, or worse, the clueless who should be using your solution, but don't even care enough to use your competitor's product.

If they only thought like you, of course, and knew what you know, then there wouldn't be a problem.

The challenge doesn't lie in getting them to know what you know. It won't help. The challenge lies in helping them see your idea through their lens, not yours. If you study the way religions and political movements spread, you can see that this is exactly how it works. Marketers of successful ideas rarely market the facts. Instead, they market stories that match the worldview of the people being marketed to.

We can't be stupid about our educational task. We can't just blurt things out willy-nilly and then decide our listeners are wrong for not joining us. People already have a mindset. We must reach into that mindset and change it. In order to do that, we must avoid putting the person on the defensive. We can't defeat them in arguments. We can't make ourselves out to be an opponent. We must be on the same side.

We cannot ignore the already existing beliefs in the other person's head. We have to show them that we share core values with them, and then help them understand what we understand.

8. Think Outside the Argument Box

There are many books on the topic of persuasion, and a lot of books on arguing. But these deal with two different things. Argumentation is about logic and facts and evidence, and works best on an audience *listening* to the argument (rather than participating in it).

Persuasion *includes* facts and logic. But it also includes the human element. Emotions, culturally-specific triggers, your rapport with each other, memories, allegiances, feelings, psychological factors, associations, subliminal influences, etc. These elements of persuasion work directly on the person you're talking to, and work best one-on-one, which is usually what most of us are doing when we talk about Islamic doctrine — we're talking personally to one friend or family member at a time.

I recommend studying *persuasion* rather than argumentation (unless you're a public speaker).

If you're arguing with people and feel stuck, it's time to add something else to your side. You're arguing on a level field — argument against argument, fact against opposing fact, logic against logic. The effort often feels futile. The argument goes around and around and doesn't seem to get anywhere. When this happens, you can add something extra to *your* side — add something outside the argument box.

You can find good ideas in books on persuasion. One such book is *Get Anyone to Do Anything and Never Feel Powerless Again* by David J. Lieberman. Here are a few ideas quoted from the book:

1. Studies show that when our self-awareness is heightened we are more easily influenced. This suggests that when we can see ourselves — literally — in a reflection, we are more persuadable. Having a conversation by a mirrored wall or reflective panel will increase your chances of influencing the person.

2. Reciprocal persuasion: Researchers found that if someone had previously persuaded you to change your mind, he would be more inclined to reciprocate by changing his attitudes about something when you ask. Similarly, if you had resisted his appeal and not changed your mind, he would often "reciprocate" by refusing to change his own mind. You can use this very easily to your advantage by saying, "I thought about what you said regarding [any previous conversation where he was explaining his point of view] and I've come to agree with your thinking. You're right."

3. Studies conclude that when a person holds an opposing view, you should adopt a two-sided argument. When you're dealing with a stubborn person, we can likely assume that he's based his opinion, at least in part, on fact. Therefore, a one-

sided argument will appear to him as if you are not taking his thinking into consideration. Consequently, in this instance, present both sides (following the rule of primacy, be sure to present your side first) and you will find him more malleable in his thinking.

I QUOTED ALL three of the ideas above from *a single page* of Lieberman's 180-page book. These kinds of ideas might help you get outside of a deadlock. They can help you continue the fight, but in a new way with an unexpected advantage. They can make your conversations more interesting and challenging for you. They can make your efforts feel less futile and more fun. And they might increase your success rate.

I'm challenging all of us to do what the teacher in *Freedom Writers* did (you'll read about her shortly), and when you can't seem to reach someone — when you seem unable to make your message penetrate — that you *find a different way* rather than simply blaming your listener or doing the same thing only more intensely. Find a way around the impasse.

Use ideas from books on salesmanship, persuasion, and influence to help you get around the obstacles interfering with your goal.

9. An Aversion to Cruelty

Richard Rorty said liberals feel an "aversion to cruelty" and that's one of the primary reasons they are a liberal in the first place. Somehow this struck me as worth remembering. I don't like to divide this issue into a "conservative versus liberal" issue because it is important to all of us, and many liberals are ardent counterjihadists (and some conservatives still don't want to believe Islamic teachings pose a danger to non-Muslims). But Rorty's idea struck a chord. One thing we're up against — one source of the resistance you run into when you begin talking to a non-Muslim about Islamic doctrine — is a strong "aversion to cruelty."

I think we will find an improved ability to reach people who have such an aversion if we understand this fundamental truth about them.

For example, you can make it perfectly clear right up front that *you* abhor cruelty, that you are against racism and treating anyone badly, that you're not a "Muslim-basher" or a "hatemonger." Make it clear you are not a mean person. These are the most likely ways they will interpret your criticism of Islam. These are the most likely ways they will try to make sense of your motivations for saying what you're saying about Islamic texts.

I'm assuming you are against cruelty, racism, and hatred. So you should make sure you vehemently express your dislike and distrust of these things. In other words, show a little *more* aversion to cruelty than they do, and talk about Islamic doctrine in a way that shows them that the reason you want to educate the world about Islamic texts is to *prevent* cruelty and inequality and bigotry.

Go out of your way to point out that you are against hating Muslims themselves, and that what you want to speak about is an ideology of intolerance and supremacism, and that thank goodness most Muslims are good enough human beings to ignore these core Islamic teachings.

You can then go on to say that unfortunately, just because many Muslims ignore these teachings, that's not the end of the issue because the Muslim children are vulnerable to recruiting. And enough Muslims do definitely believe in Islam, so an uneducated population of non-Muslims is vulnerable to infiltration, deceit, the removal of freedoms, and ultimately to subjugation.

You might not want to go that far (subjugation) because most people at this beginning level of innocence about Islam don't think that's possible.

We should only tell as much truth as can be believed. Give people a chance to come to grips with the horrible implications of what you're saying. Don't overwhelm them or make them recoil from the information.

If you can "come from" the aversion you have to cruelty, you may gain their ear. You will at least help prevent them from putting you in a "racism" box and perhaps they'll become confused enough about you to listen. I'm not recommending you deliberately confuse people, but help them realize they can't characterize you the way they thought, and if they don't have a way to easily characterize you, they may simply listen to you out of curiosity.

When you can see you've aroused their curiosity, help them see that concessions to Sharia will ultimately lead to cruelty, even though at first it may seem tolerant and fair-minded to give them the special accommodations they demand.

If you can do this, your listener will walk away from the conversation with a whole new perspective. It will make them more open to information about the disturbing nature of Islamic doctrine. And hopefully it will lead them to investigate the issue for themselves.

If they ask you more about it later, do your best to encourage them to read the Koran. That should be the first step for all of us.

10. Preemptive Ideological Strike

Yesterday I was on a lunch break with a new hire at work. I've been working with him for three days, and we had good rapport (this is an important point to remember). We had a mutual feeling of liking and respect. He is a good man. We were on a break and he was talking about religion. We were getting to know each other. He told me he reads widely on many religions. So naturally I asked him, "What do you know about Islam?"

"Not much," he said. "I'd really like to know more."

"Well you're in luck," I said, "because I know a lot about it."

I had been hoping for a perfect opportunity like this. He'd already told me he was politically "progressive," and we hadn't broached the topic of Islam yet, but I knew it would happen eventually. And I had been thinking it would be better to talk about it casually — before we were disagreeing on something specific. And since I already had good rapport with him, I thought now would be a great time.

I began like this: "I started reading about Islam right after 9-11."

"A lot of people did," he said supportively, "I remember Korans were selling well."

"Yeah, I wanted to know what the story was. So many things were being said about Islam — you know, that it was all about peace, but then you had terrorists quoting the Koran, and I didn't know what to think about it all. I eventually read the Koran cover to cover, and that was no easy task, let me tell you. That was one of the most boring books I've ever read."

He looked at me like maybe I was joking.

"I'm serious. It was repetitive and didn't really say much. Or at least it didn't at first. But the last fourth of the book got really interesting. It changed totally. Do you know how the Koran was written?"

"No."

"Muhammad got these revelations from an angel named Gabriel. He was living in Mecca at the time, and there were a lot of religions in Mecca, including Judaism and Christianity, and he seemed to pick up a lot of their ideas. Anyway, the Koran is just a collection of Muhammad's revelations. That is all that's in there. The whole thing was dictated by Muhammad. Once in awhile, for the rest of his life, Islamic history says he received revelations from the angel, Gabriel.

"But his revelations changed at some point. See, at first Muhammad was just one guy among many in a very religiously tolerant place, and he preached tolerance and non-violence. Most of his revelations were about what hell was like and what paradise was like, and how if you don't believe in Allah and if you don't believe Muhammad was Allah's prophet, you were going to hell.

"After 13 years, he gained 150 converts. But Muhammad was always criticizing the other religions of Mecca, and the Meccans resented it, and eventually made his life pretty unpleasant there, so he moved to Medina, where he had some followers, and they set Muhammad up as a kind of leader of their gang."

He looked at me kind of skeptically so I said, "And this history I'm telling you is from *Islamic* sources, not writings by people who don't like Is-

lam. Anyway, so the Muslims started raiding caravans going to Mecca, since the Meccans were his
enemies now, and the enemies of Islam. Muhammad and his believers would raid the caravans, kill
the people, and take their stuff. Well, sometimes
they would capture some of the people alive and
hold them for ransom.

"All of a sudden, Muhammad started getting a
lot more people interested in joining Islam."

My workmate smiled at this. He understood
that there is a certain kind of person who would
want to get in on the booty from these raids.

"Yeah, it was a pretty good gig," I said. "They
started accumulating some wealth. And Muhammad's little group of followers was growing into an
army. Eventually they took over the city of Medina.

"Around this time is when the revelations
changed," I said ominously.

"What do you mean?" he asked. He was definitely interested now. We were not arguing. Not
at all. The feeling of contention was completely
absent in this conversation. He wanted to know
about Islam, and I was telling him what I found
out. I just talked to him like a person who found
the whole thing surprising and interesting and
wants to share it.

I kept going: "Well, the revelations started becoming less tolerant and more violent. That's what
I mean about the last part of the Koran getting

interesting. I mean interesting in the sense that it got rid of the confusion I had to begin with."

"Like you, I have also read a lot about different religions, especially Buddhism, Taoism, and Christianity. Before I learned about Islam, I figured most religions were pretty much the same, at least as far as basic principles go."

He was nodding his head.

"You know what I mean? I thought religions were always started by a wise, kind person who gathers people around him because they can see he is wise. And he spends his life helping people, and then his followers build a religion based on his teachings.

"So when I was reading the Koran, I almost couldn't believe what I was reading. This was totally different than any religion I had ever heard of. Muhammad *led* the raids on the caravans? He *killed* people?! The *founder* of the religion was doing these things? I was blown away.

"At one point, Muhammad personally oversaw the beheading of around 600 men. He tortured a rabbi to find out where a particular group of Jews had hidden their gold. I mean, can you imagine Buddha or Jesus doing that? I couldn't believe it! Muhammad actually ordered the assassination of people who criticized Islam."

Lights were going on in my workmate's head. He said, "That's like that guy who wrote 'Satanic Verses.'"

"Right! They're just following Muhammad's example. In fact, it says in the Koran that Muhammad is a model for human behavior and followers should try to be like Muhammad."

Then I anticipated what I know from experience people will think of: That other religious books have violence in them and we shouldn't pick on Islam. So I said, "But you know how the Bible has lots of different kinds of writings? Some are violent and some are peaceful, right?"

"Yeah," he said, nodding like he was just thinking the same thing.

"And if you have contradictions in the Bible, it's not really a big deal because it was written over such a long time by so many people. Well, that's not the case with the Koran. It actually says in the Koran itself what to do with its own contradictions.

"It really had to deal with this issue, because if you think about it, there is Muhammad preaching tolerance and non-violence, and his believers know those teachings already, and then the revelations change pretty dramatically. It was very noticeable to everyone. So Allah says in the Koran in one of the revelations that if something I say contradicts something I've said earlier, the newer stuff overwrites the older stuff."

He grasped right away what that meant. "So the more violent parts cancel out the peaceful parts?"

"Yes, exactly. Isn't that mind-blowing? I mean, what a shock. But you know, ever since I read the Koran, I'm no longer confused by the news. I used to wonder what the hell is wrong with the Middle East. Why can't they seem to work out their differences and just get along? I mean, seriously, how long has this been going on? Now I realize that the Muslims really can't. They can't work things out with the Jews and still remain Muslims! And other stuff, like hijackings and kidnappings and suicide bombers started to seem not so bewildering any more."

I had just given my workmate a lot to think about. So I said, "Well, we probably ought to get back to work." And as we were on our way back, I changed the topic of conversation to something else. I didn't want to "sell past the close" and I didn't want to appear to be a fanatic. I decided right then that I will not to bring up the subject again with him. I will maintain rapport with him, and just let him digest.

I feel pretty confident he'll ask me a question about Islam at some future time.

I didn't think at the time about making a "preemptive strike." I was just having an interesting conversation. But the more I thought about it afterwards, the more profitable this approach appeared to me. If we could have these kinds of conversations *before* we're in an argument, we could establish our position as the one who knows about this topic, and establish their position as a curious student. And we could bypass the whole political argument. We could prevent our listeners from stubbornly digging into their trenches on this issue (where no minds can be changed).

We'd have more influence, in other words. I feel confident he will never listen to any information about Islam the same way again.

The approach would probably only work on people who don't already know that you know something about Islam — people you haven't already had conversations with about it. You could just casually ask, when the opportunity presents itself (and when your rapport is strong, and when you are alone so it could be a private, one-on-one conversation), "What do you know about Islam?" or "Do you know much about Islam?"

Your chances are really good that they won't know anything. And that creates a wonderful opportunity.

11. The Enemy of Us All

A growing movement in Europe is explicitly anti-Muslim. This is both good news and bad news. The good news is the problems inherent in orthodox Islamic encroachment into Western democracies is being discussed publicly. The bad news is that some of the most outspoken are white supremacists.

For those of us who are not racists but who see the growing threat of Islamic encroachment, the white supremacists are a problem.

People on the other side, the multiculturalists and the Muslims and many of the most ardent anti-conservatives see anyone who speaks out against Islam or tries to educate people about Islamic doctrine as racists and white supremacists and fascists. And, in fact, there *are* some fascists who speak out against Islam. But we're not all fascists, of course. We're not all white supremacists. We're not all racists. Not by a long shot.

What is racism? It is an overgeneralization. It says because *some* members of the racial group have a particular characteristic, *all* members of the race have that characteristic.

The blind multiculturalists also overgeneralize when they say *all* people in the counterjihad movement are racists. They are making exactly the same mistake they are accusing us of making (that most of us are not making). That is, since a few of us who are working to curtail Islam's expansion are racists, then anyone who says they don't like Islamic doctrine is a racist. It's the same mistake. It's an overgeneralization.

And even those of us participating in the counterjihad who are not racists often make the same mistake against both Muslims and multiculturalists by thinking that all Muslims want to kill non-Muslims, or all multiculturalists are just naïve fools.

Another example of the same mistake is "white guilt" (as it is known in America) or "post-colonial guilt" (as it is known in Europe). This guilt is being exploited by many orthodox Muslims. It makes us less able to defend ourselves, and the source of the guilt is the same mistake: Overgeneralization.

America had slaves. That was wrong. But should I feel guilty about that? I've never owned a slave or endorsed the idea. I have no idea if any of my ancestors did, either, and even if they *did*, it wouldn't matter. Any crime committed by my ancestors does not make *me* guilty. And any bad action taken by someone with the same skin color as me does not make me guilty either.

This guilt — which allows orthodox Muslims to get away with things they wouldn't be able to get away with otherwise — is caused by an overgeneralization (that all white people are cruel or guilty and have amends to make).

One of the things non-Muslims dislike the most about the content of Islamic teachings is "kafir hatred," which is, of course, the same mistake yet again. The Koran says Muslims are the best of people and non-Muslims are the worst of people. These are overgeneralizations.

On all sides, we see the same mistake, and it makes any productive conversation almost impossible. If you believe you do not make this mistake, I suggest to you that you're probably wrong.

It's a natural mental error human brains are prone to make.

How can we get out of this mess? How can we have productive conversations about Islamic doctrine with our fellow non-Muslims? How can we help educate those who are against our cause? The answer is to *be specific*, and insist that others be specific too.

We in the counterjihad are talking about Islamic *doctrine*. We must make it absolutely clear that we are talking about doctrine, not people. We are talking about *Islamic ideology*, not Muslims. When we're talking about a Muslim, we need to speak about a particular Muslim. Our overgeneralizations usually come from talking about a group of people rather than a specific person or an ideology. Any group of people contains individuals. Individuals will be different from each other, will have different levels of belief, will have different levels of commitment to the ideology, will have different understandings and familiarity with the ideology, and will have different characteristics from each other.

And we can speak specifically about Sharia law. This is a very effective way to avoid overgeneralizing.

We can also make a clear distinction between the different *kinds* of Muslims: Orthodox and heterodox, for example, or Jihad-embracing Muslims and Jihad-rejecting Muslims, Practicing Muslims versus MINOs (Muslim in Name Only).

Do whatever you can to be as specific as possible and avoid overgeneralizations. We must be eternally vigilant with our own thoughts, with our own speaking and writing, and we must carefully and deliberately expose the error when others make it.

And when we're pointing it out in others, we should avoid ridiculing them for making the error. The tendency to overgeneralize is a natural by-product of the brain's functional design and requires constant vigilance from all of us to prevent our brains from making this error.

Overgeneralization gets in the way of good communication. It interferes with accurate thinking. It impairs our ability to solve problems. Overgeneralization is the enemy of us all.

12. Training Course for Citizen Warriors

To help you in your quest to educate your fellow non-Muslims, I highly recommend *The Dale Carnegie Course: Effective Communications and Human Relations*. It's the perfect training for a citizen warrior.

I took the course about twenty-three years ago, and it made a huge difference. And it recently occurred to me that an important factor in my ability to educate people face-to-face is the training I got all those years ago — training available to you now.

Our most important task is to educate people. This requires an ability to persuade, to successfully connect with people, to organize your thoughts and get them across clearly, and ideally, to keep your stress level low. The *Dale Carnegie Course* will help you in all of these areas.

The training course takes place over a period of twelve weeks, one night per week, three and a half hours per night. And every night each participant gives two short speeches. That's a lot of practice. And you get excellent coaching from the course leader. Of all the public speaking training I have gotten — and I've gotten quite a lot — by far the very best was the *Dale Carnegie Course*.

People graduate from the course with the ability to really communicate, not just the ability to make good gestures or use vocal variety or any of the other things a lot of public speaking programs focus on. The *Dale Carnegie Course* goes right to the core of communication and connection and will teach you how to get your message across in a way that penetrates.

Dale Carnegie originally created a class to help people conquer their fear of speaking in public. But he noticed that most of the problems people talked about in their speeches were *human relations* problems. He thought he might teach some basic principles of human relations along with public speaking in the same course. So he looked around for a book on human relations but couldn't find one he thought was good enough, so he wrote one:

How to Win Friends and Influence People, which became one of the bestselling books of all time. You will use that book and learn to apply those time-tested principles during the course.

One of the great things about the *Dale Carnegie Course* is learning to express yourself more freely. You'll gain that elusive quality known as charisma. Even if you are already charismatic, you'll become even more so.

The course is especially good for people who have a fear of public speaking. You'll start out sitting in front of the class with three other people and all you have to do is answer the course leader's questions. It's very easy. Even if you're afraid to speak in public, this isn't stressful.

The course slowly progresses from there, step-by-step, allowing you to remain comfortable all along the way until you're standing up there by yourself giving a prepared speech and having no trouble whatsoever doing it.

Many famous people have taken the course and say it changed their lives — Lee Iacocca, Mary Kay Ash, Lyndon B. Johnson, Ann Landers, Chuck Norris, Annette Benning, Joe DiMaggio, Mickey Mantle, and the list goes on and on.

I would recommend this course to anyone, but it is especially valuable for those of us who wish to awaken our fellow non-Muslims about Islam's ideology. You'll get the tools you need to be effective.

And I have something else to say. Although my focus here is making you a better citizen warrior, the *Dale Carnegie Course* will be personally good for you — you'll be happier and more expressive, you will have more personal freedom of expression, and it will be great for your ability to bring people to our side.

Think about it. It's a substantial investment of time and money. But you will not regret it. I think you will, like me, come to think of it as the best money you've ever spent and the best investment of time you've ever made.

The *Dale Carnegie Course* is available almost anywhere. Check out their website to find a course in your area.

The first evening of the course is free for everyone. If you like it, you can sign up. If not, you got a free class. And they actually teach you something useful the first night. And no, you are not put on the spot or asked to give a speech in the first class.

One of the most prominent features of the military is constant training. The military never stops training its soldiers. And we *citizen* warriors should also constantly focus on training, on getting better, on improving our skills, and the *Dale Carnegie Course* is one of the best ways to do that.

13. Get Motivated to Think Outside the Argument Box by Watching "Freedom Writers"

I just watched the movie, *Freedom Writers* for the second time. It's a good movie and a true story. But this time I realized the movie illustrates something I continually hammer on: If you can't reach somebody, one possibility is to blame *them* for the failure of your message to penetrate. Another possibility is to look at yourself, look at the way you communicate, and try to find other ways.

The first approach leaves you the victim of the mindset of other people. The second approach will give you power, will give you *ability*, and will open your mind to possibly finding or creating ways to get through.

Your ability to think up or learn new ways to do something is greatly facilitated by an open mind. In order to relieve the cognitive dissonance regarding why people seem to stubbornly refuse to understand even the most basic things about Islamic doctrine, many of us in the counterjihad movement write them off. We've all done it. We explain our setbacks by blaming our listeners, and while that's a perfectly understandable response, that kind of explanation leaves us *less capable* of overcoming our obstacles.

You make it more possible to overcome the obstacles if you think differently about these setbacks.

Think of it this way: You have obstacles to overcome and you need to find a way to become more creative. You need to find a way to get around the obstacles. And you don't have to think the obstacles are anyone's fault, so there's no one to be angry with. This is just the way it is. All you need to focus on is finding a way to penetrate their ignorance. Find a way to get basic information about Islamic doctrine understood by people who don't know it yet.

It helps your own attitude to think of yourself as being *in training*. Your own motivation and the obstacles you're running into are combining to teach you what you need to learn to reach people, to connect with people, and to help them understand and become motivated to learn more, just like the teacher in *Freedom Writers*.

The teacher was fresh out of college, very idealistic, and her first job was at a school with forced integration. She was an English teacher and her ninth-grade students were basically the academic failures of the school. They had been passed along in the school system for a long time, and they were almost entirely uneducated, mostly members of gangs who had been bussed in from another part of town, and they didn't care about education or graduating or anything else a teacher might need her students to care about to motivate them to listen to her.

She was frustrated that they didn't care about what she wanted to teach them. They were openly hostile toward her. Does this sound familiar? Have you felt the same way? Do you sometimes feel people don't care what you have to teach and they are openly hostile to you?

The teacher went to get help from the administrators of the school, and they basically told her, "don't beat your head against the wall, these kids are not going to learn, and the best you can do is to try to instill some kind of discipline."

She talked to other teachers, and got pretty much the same response. They explained their failure to reach the students, their failure to get through, by blaming the students or blaming the students' circumstances, or their culture, or whatever. All these explanations tend to close the mind to finding a way to get through. It's an attempt to explain failure rather than an attempt to solve the problem.

Many of us are making the same mistake. We talk to our friends and family about Islamic doctrine and meet resistance. Many of them react with anger and seem impervious to anything we have the say. They have preconceived notions about our message (or of the "kind of people" who communicate that sort of message).

This is what the students did in the movie (and in real life). They looked at this young white teacher, and they felt *no connection* whatsoever with her. They knew for a fact she didn't understand what they were dealing with every day — the violence, the fear, the uncertainty, the pressure to conform to the rules that have already been set up within the gangs and within their neighborhoods, the pressures from their peers.

This young teacher had no clue about how things worked. She didn't know the rules: If a student rejects their own racial group in their neighborhoods — if they are Hispanic but don't want to be involved in wars with the neighboring Koreans, for example — their own Hispanic neighbors and relatives will become hostile to them, and they'll have no way to protect themselves from the hostility they'll get from the Koreans either.

Those students had difficult choices to make. They lived in a difficult environment, and they looked at their teacher, who was trying to teach them things in which they had no interest, and they saw no relevance to their lives. She could not reach them.

So instead of continuing to try reaching them using the same method and continually failing, or alternatively, giving up and blaming the students for her inability to reach them, she tried a third option: She tried a *different way* around the obstacles.

When what you are doing is not working, *try something else*. It's usually a good policy.

So what did she do? She found different ways of reaching them. For example, she tried to get some good books for them to read, but the school didn't want the academic failures of the school to use those books because the school administrators "knew" the students would simply destroy the books because they didn't care about learning.

The teacher wanted to get her students interested in learning, but she couldn't get any books they'd be interested in reading, so she got a second job in order to buy books she thought would interest her students. It's not right, she shouldn't have had to do it, but she didn't limit herself to "the way things ought to be." She thought outside the box. She focused on her goal.

She caught one of the students passing around a note in the classroom one day. But it wasn't really a note, it was a drawing of one of the students that exaggerated his racial features and made fun of him. The class had been passing it around and giggling.

The teacher got angry. She said this is how the Holocaust started. She remembered seeing a similar drawing in a museum that exaggerated Jewish racial features.

Then she found out most of them didn't know what the Holocaust was! And because she had not closed her mind, because — and only because — she was actively *looking* for a way to reach them, she found it. She realized *this* might be something that would interest them.

She said, "You think *your* gangs are tough? They don't even come close to what the Nazis did. That was a gang to reckon with!"

She convinced the school superintendent to give her permission to take her students on a field

trip to a Holocaust memorial (the school administrators rejected the idea, but the superintendent
gave her the go-ahead, which really angered the
school administrators).

But the teacher was right: The students were
fascinated. After the field trip, she set up a dinner
with her students and invited three actual Holocaust survivors. The students talked with these
survivors and asked them questions. They were interested, they were connecting, they were *learning.*

Then the teacher (with her own money again)
bought everybody in the class a copy of *The Diary of
Anne Frank.* They became even more fascinated.
Intrigued. Interested in learning. And interested in
listening to this teacher and what she had to say.

She thought creatively. She *found* a way to reach
them.

This is what we must do. When we can't reach
someone with our message, our response should
be, "What can I do *differently* that will allow me to
reach this person? What different approach could I
use that *would* penetrate? What approach could I
use that would get this person interested in learning about Islam?"

After reading *The Diary of Anne Frank,* the students were in awe at the courage of the woman
who risked her life to hide Anne Frank and her
family for all that time.

So the teacher suggested as one of their English assignments that everyone in the class write
a letter to that woman.

The students said, "We should send our letters to the woman, if she's still alive." The teacher was just thinking of it as a writing assignment and hadn't considered actually *sending* the letters. But the students said, "Why not? In fact, why not invite her here so we can meet her?"

The teacher was taken by surprise. She stammered, "I don't know how to reach her, I don't know if she can even travel. She might be too *old* to travel," but the students were so excited by the idea, the teacher looked into it.

And she was able to find the woman who harbored Anne Frank and her family, and this woman was moved by the letters the students wrote, *so she came to the United States*, to Long Beach where the students went to school, and talked with them.

It changed their lives.

If you are committed to doing the one thing that needs to be done — that is, awakening your fellow non-Muslims to basic information about Islamic doctrine — I invite you to suspend you're already-existing explanations for why you can't get through to some people, and open *your* mind.

Decide that you will *find* a way. Decide you will learn about persuasion. Decide you will seek new ideas about influencing people. Decide you will overcome the obstacles. Decide to try new things besides what you've tried already that didn't work.

Sure, being more forceful is one option. Being more frustrated is another option. But neither of those work very well. What *other* ways can you try? How many different ways can you try?

And when you find new ways I urge you, I plead with you, to share those ways with your fellow counterjihadists. Tell us what you tried and how it worked. Go to this blog and share with us:

TalkAboutIslamAmongNonMuslims.blogspot.com

Let's share our ideas and experiences with each other and let's all get better at this.

Watch the movie *Freedom Writers* and get inspired to find new ways to reach people. Make the assumption that it *can* be done, and don't stop until you find a way.

14. Criticize Islamic Texts By Talking About Scientology.

When someone you're talking to turns against the idea of criticizing Islamic ideology, switch to talking about Scientology. Talk about Scientology's *Fair Game* policy for awhile, and once your listener agrees with you that the policy is unacceptable, make these points:

1. Not all religions are the same.

2. Religious doctrine should not be free from scrutiny.

3. There is a useful division we can make between the *political* teachings of a religion and the *religious* teachings of that religion.

In case you don't know about Scientology's Fair Game policy, here it is in a nutshell: It is a written doctrine of the Church of Scientology that enemies of Scientology are "fair game" and may be (in the words of Scientology's founder), "deprived of property or injured by any means by any Scientologist without any discipline of the Scientologist. May be tricked, sued, lied to, or destroyed." Anyone who leaves Scientology is considered an enemy of Scientology. They actually consider the person to be an enemy of *Mankind* since Scientology is considered to be the only thing that can save humanity.

The Fair Game policy has been carried out by the Church of Scientology many times, often destroying the lives of former Scientologists (apostates), and Scientology's criminal actions (and its written policies supporting those actions) have often been documented in court. You can read more about this online. Start at the "Scientology Critical Information Directory" and the "Suppressive Person Defense League."

Islam has successfully gathered a cloak of protection around it, making it difficult to talk about this subject with many people. But people do not have the same knee-jerk defense of Scientology, and yet many of Scientology's teachings are similar to Islam's. So learn something about Scientology, and when you meet resistance when talking about Islam, switch to talking about Scientology.

Once you've made some good points about Scientology, come back around and make the same points about Islam. I think you'll find this a powerful new strategy.

15. More on Using Scientology to Criticize Islam

I'm reading a biography of L. Ron Hubbard, the founder of Scientology which I heartily recommend to you, entitled, *Bare-Faced Messiah*. When you encounter resistance to your criticism of Islamic doctrine, you can sidestep to talking about Scientology, which has many parallels with Islam's core principles and policies. Nobody seems to mind when you criticize Scientology (except a Scientologist, of course).

You can criticize something about Scientology, and then say the same thing about Islam, and if someone gives you a bad time about it, you can ask, "Why is it okay to talk about Scientology but not Islam?"

It is no more racist to talk about Islam than Scientology, for example. And you can make that point very effectively and very reasonably, and thereby greatly reduce the flak you take for doing something everyone in free nations should be engaged in: Religious and political criticism and free discussion.

What's the point of free speech if we aren't exercising it?

Anyway, below are eight excerpts from *Bare-Faced Messiah*. As you read, I'd like you to consider what a conversation might be like if you said, "I was reading something about Scientology today that really surprised me." Then talk about it for a bit. And then say, "It reminded me of something very similar about Islam." And talk about that for a bit. This is received with less resistance than talking about Islam only. Give it a try and you'll see what I mean. Here are the eight excerpts from the book:

1. "While Hubbard (L. Ron Hubbard) was skirmishing with the FBI, he was also tightening his grip on the Scientology movement and urging his followers to take action against anyone attempting to practice Scientology outside the control of the 'church'. He derided apostates as 'squirrels' and recommended merciless litigation to drive them out of business. 'The law can be used very easily to

harass, and enough harassment on somebody who is simply on the thin edge anyway, well knowing that he is not authorized, will generally be sufficient to cause his professional decease,' he wrote in one of his interminable bulletins, casually adding, 'If possible, of course, ruin him utterly.'

"In the same bulletin he offered the benefit of his advice to any Scientologists unlucky enough to be arrested. They were to instantly file a $100,000 civil damages suit for molestation of 'a Man of God going about his business', then go on the offensive 'forcefully, artfully, and arduously' and cause 'blue flames to dance on the courthouse roof until everybody has apologized profusely'. The only way to defend anything, Hubbard wrote, was to attack. 'If you ever forget that, you will lose every battle you are ever engaged in.' It was a philosophy to which he would adhere ardently all his life..."

2. "The same month as the Freedom Congress, the Central Intelligence Agency opened a file, No. 156409, on L. Ron Hubbard and his organization. CIA agents trawled through police, revenue, credit and property records to try and unravel Hubbard's tangled corporate affairs. It was a task of Herculean difficulty, for the Church of Scientology was a cryptic maze of *ad hoc* corporations. The printed notepaper of the Academy of Scientology gave only a hint of its labyrinthine structure — on the left-hand side of the page was a list of no less than seventeen associated organizations, ranging from

the American Society for Disaster Relief to the Society of Consulting Ministers.

"Agents traced a considerable amount of property owned either by Hubbard, his wife, son, or one of the daunting number of 'churches' with which they were associated, but the report quickly became bogged down in a tangle of names and addresses: 'The Academy of Religious Arts and Sciences is currently engaged as a school for ministers of religion which at the present time possesses approximately thirty to forty students. The entire course consists of $1500 to $1800 worth of actual classroom studies...The public office is located at 1810-12 19th Street N.W. The corporations rent the entire building...

"'The Hubbard Guidance Center, located at 2315 15th Street, N.W., occupies the entire building which consists of three floors and which was purchased by the SUBJECT Organization. The center also rents farm property located somewhere along Colesville Road in Silver Spring, Maryland, on a short-term lease. The center formerly operated a branch office at 8609 Flower Avenue, Silver Spring, Maryland. In addition to the Silver Spring operation, the center has a working agreement with the Founding Church of Scientology of New York, which holds classes at Studio 847, Carnegie Hall, 154 West 57th Street, New York City. Churches of this denomination number in excess of one hundred in the United States...'"

3. "While he was still in Melbourne, Hubbard received an urgent telephone call from Washington with some bad news. Nibs (Hubbard's son, Ron Hubbard, Jr.), he was told, had 'blown'. To Scientologists, 'blowing the org' (leaving the church) was one of the worst crimes in the book: it was almost unbelievable that the highly-placed son and namesake of the founder would take such a step...

"[Nibs] failed to take into account the fact that his father would automatically view his defection as an act of treachery..."

4. "Returning to a familiar theme, Hubbard urged his followers to defend Scientology by attacking its opponents: 'If attacked on some vulnerable point by anyone or anything or any organization, always find or manufacture enough threat against them to cause them to sue for peace...Don't ever defend, always attack. Don't ever do nothing. Unexpected attacks in the rear of the enemy's front ranks work best.'"

5. "'It was not really possible to question what was going on,' explained David Mayo, a New Zealander and a long-time member of the Sea Org (the headquarters of Scientology worldwide, which was a small fleet of ships), 'because you were never sure who you could really trust. To question anything Hubbard did or said was an offense and you never knew if you would be reported. Most of the crew were afraid that if they expressed any disagree-

ment with what was going on they would be kicked out of Scientology. That was something absolutely untenable to most people, something you never wanted to consider. That was much more terrifying than anything that might happen to you in the Sea Org.

"'We tried not to think too hard about his behavior. It was not rational much of the time, but to even consider such a thing was a discreditable thought and you couldn't allow yourself to have a discreditable thought. One of the questions in a sec-check (a security check, using a lie detector, which is done frequently throughout the organization) was, "Have you ever had any unkind thoughts about LRH?" and you could get into very serious trouble if you had. So you tried hard not to.'"

6. "Now sixty-two, Hubbard was also beginning to ponder his place in posterity. The Church of Scientology had been swift to make use of the recently enacted Freedom of Information Act, which had revealed that government agencies held a daunting amount of material about Scientology and its founder in their files, much of it less than flattering. Hubbard, who had never been fettered by convention or strict observance of the law, conceived a simple, but startlingly audacious, plan to improve his own image and that of his church for the benefit of future generations of Scientologists. All that needed to be done, he decided, was to

infiltrate the agencies concerned, steal the relevant files and either destroy or launder any damaging information they contained. To a man who had founded both a church and a private navy this was a perfectly feasible scheme. The operation was given the code name Snow White — two words that would figure ever more prominently over the next few months in the communications between the Guardian's Office in Los Angeles and the Commodore's (Hubbard's) hiding place in Queens, New York."

7. "At six o'clock on the morning of 8 July 1977, 134 FBI agents armed with search warrants and sledgehammers, simultaneously broke into the offices of the Church of Scientology in Washington and Los Angeles and carted away 48,149 documents. They would reveal an astonishing espionage system which spanned the United States and penetrated some of the highest offices in the land."

8. This is a quote from the government sentencing memorandum on Mary Sue Hubbard and the others, October 1978: "The crime committed by these defendants is of a breadth and scope previously unheard of. No building, office, desk or file was safe from their snooping and prying. No individual or organization was free from their despicable conspiratorial minds. The tools of their trade were miniature transmitters, lock picks, sec-

ret codes, forged credentials, and any other device they found necessary to carry out their conspiratorial schemes. It is interesting to note that the founder of their organization, unindicted co-conspirator L. Ron Hubbard, wrote in his dictionary entitled *Modern Management Technology Defined* that 'Truth is what is true for you.' Thus, with the founder's blessings, they could wantonly commit perjury as long as it was in the interests of Scientology."

Okay, enough quotes from Hubbard's biography. All of the above could have been pulled straight out of the Muslim Brotherhood's playbook. Go on the offensive. Attack anybody who impedes your goals. Use the courts to harass. Be merciless until people are apologizing profusely. Invoke "freedom of religion" as a cloak of protection. Create lots of different important-sounding organizations, and make the names seem mainstream and respectable, and try not to use your own religion's name in the title to throw people off your trail and to make it seem like a coalition of many religions. Create a "labyrinthine structure" of organizations to make it almost impossible for anyone to follow the money. Consider apostates as enemies to be destroyed.

Criticism of the religion or the founder is completely forbidden, resulting in unthinking, uncritical (and therefore fanatical) followers. Scientologists use a lie detector. Islam uses Allah, who knows every thought you think and will judge you and punish you accordingly.

The list of similarities goes on and on: Infiltrate government agencies in order to protect and promote the religion. And lying is allowed if it is done to further the goals of the religion.

Begin to talk about Scientology and Islam together and your conversations will be more interesting, less contentious, and far more productive. With this new strategy, we should be able to reach more people in less time.

The best biography of Hubbard to read for a good overview of the basic Scientology doctrine is called *Messiah or Madman?*

16. How to Get Listening Leverage

One of the most powerful things you can do to increase your ability to persuade is to do physically helpful things for the person you want to persuade. To be kind in *action* — not making a show of it, but just doing it. Nothing says, "I'm on your side," with as much impact as a genuinely kind deed.

Everybody can use some help now and then. Just look for small things. Once you start looking, you'll find lots of opportunities to help.

Not only will this feel good, and not only will it be good for your health (because of the "helper's high" kind acts will give you), but for our purposes here, it also puts the other person in a position of obligation to you.

Most people have a natural desire to reciprocate kindness. They will want to discharge their feeling of obligation to you, and *you* have a great deal of influence over *how* they discharge it.

You can ask them to watch a DVD or read an article or watch an online video, for example. You can say, "I know you don't like this stuff, but just do it for me, okay?" If you have built up a sufficient feeling of obligation toward you, they will do it.

Doing kind, thoughtful things also makes them see you as a kind, thoughtful person, which helps prevent them from thinking of you as a "hater" or a "racist." This will help reduce their resistance to your influence.

Are you having a difficult time getting through to someone? Try gaining some listening leverage.

17. Compare Islam to Bushido.

I received an interesting email from the woman I told you about earlier who calls herself Western Feminista. She was struck by the strange similarity between Islam and Bushido.

I thought we could use this in the same way as comparing Islam with Scientology, in the sense that we may be able to get around some of the defensiveness non-Muslims have about Islam by talking about similar teachings in other religions. Here are a few of the similarities Western Feminista found:

Blind Submission:

Devotion to the Emperor (as a direct descendant of the Sun Goddess, Amaterasu Omikami) and the view that the Emperor was an earthly agent of divine origin. His decisions and judgments were, by default, moral and legal.

Muslims also revere Muhammad, the directly chosen Prophet of Allah (God). He will sit next to Allah interceding on behalf of believers on Judgment Day. It is his dictation of the words of Allah that make up the Koran that all Muslims must adhere to. His utterings are by default, moral and legal.

Humiliation and Shame:

The notions of "saving face" and the avoidance of shame have also been an integral part of Japanese culture for centuries. To admit one's wrongdoings, or worse the wrongdoings of an ancestor, would be a disgrace according to the belief in filial piety.

Lower-ranking soldiers were often beaten for the "crime" of serving a superior's rice too slowly, and sick and wounded soldiers were treated with disgust. (Infringement of the Laws of War and Ethics [January 1945]: "Many incapacitated soldiers, with a good chance of recovery, have been disposed of on the grounds that they are useless to the Emperor. A-17 Division Order commands medical officers to dispose of any sick and wounded who become a liability.") Perceived insults from Allied prisoners were met with executions, and attempts to "shame" POWs by forcing them to bow, fight for food, etc., were routinely used. Women civilians were "shamed" by being used as "comfort women."

Islam is also a Shame/Honor-based culture — obsessed with keeping face, guarding against the threat of humiliation and over-the-top reactions to the slightest perceived insult. An excellent example is the Mo-toon worldwide frothing-at-the-mouth scenario, Theo Van Gough, the film "Submission," Geert Wilders' stand against Islamification, a fatwa issued against Pokemon Toys...the list is innumerable and is growing daily.

Dhimmis are "shamed" by having to pay protection tax (jizya). Women are subjugated in the name of "honor" daily.

Free Thought Banned:

In Bushido, the Confucian precepts also set the parameters for a samurai's unquestioning obedience to his daimyo. Within the Confucian context, a "Just War" was any undertaking that the ruler sought to fulfill. They could not be questioned by anyone because that would demonstrate disrespect for authority and a questioning of the authority's divine judgment.

In Islam..."the verses of the Koran and the Sunnah summon people in general (with the most eloquent expression and the clearest exposition) to jihad, to warfare, to the armed forces, and all means of land and sea fighting." Those who can only find excuses, however, have been warned of extremely dreadful punishments and Allah has described them with the most unfortunate of names. He has reprimanded them for their cowardice and lack of spirit, and castigated them for their weakness and truancy. In this world, they will be surrounded by dishonor and in the next they will be surrounded by the fire from which they shall not escape though they may possess much wealth. The weaknesses of abstention and evasion of jihad are regarded by Allah as one of the major sins, and one of the seven sins that guarantee failure. (That is a quote from Al-Banna.)

We can also look to Islamic leaders for backup:

"Keep on fighting for the application of Islamic law. If this state and nation wants to become great, safe, and at peace then it has to return to Islam one hundred percent without bargaining. If not, then it will be destroyed." (Abu Bakar Bashir, spiritual leader of the Indonesian Mujahideen.)

"I am one of the servants of Allah. We do our duty of fighting for the sake of the religion of Allah. It is also our duty to send a call to all the people of the world to enjoy this great light and to embrace Islam and experience the happiness in Islam. Our primary mission is nothing but the furthering of this religion." (Osama bin Laden, May 1998.)

R-E-S-P-E-C-T:

Bushido also stressed respect for others, however, the term "others" was very elusive and often manipulated to mean almost anyone or only a select few. POWs being held by the Japanese Imperial Army were taken on death marches, starved, beaten, beheaded, shot and certainly not respected...the mere fact that they had surrendered sent them to the bottom of the food chain.

We have seen lots of examples put forward by Islamic apologists stating the same thing — that Islam is a peaceful religion that accepts women, Christians and Jews with respect...the passages from the Koran are too many to show here that is not the case...

War as a means to an end:

Bushido sees war as an act that could purify the self, the nation, and ultimately the whole world. Within this framework, the supreme sacrifice of life itself was regarded as the purest of accomplishments. "Do not live in shame as a prisoner. Die,

and leave no ignominious crime behind you."
Yamamoto Tsunetomo's Hagakure (1710)

Ritual suicide (seppuku) was preferred over a life of shame (defeat), and was adopted as a means of war by the Japanese Imperial Army. (Kamikaze tactic during WWII — this was also consistent with the Bushido Code's requirement of self-sacrifice.)

The idea that war is a way of "purifying" the whole world is another area where Islam agrees — the whole globe should become Islamic. Islam means submission, and so the House of Islam includes those nations that have submitted to Islamic rule, which is to say those nations ruled by Sharia law. The rest of the world, which has not accepted Sharia law and so is not in a state of submission, exists in a state of rebellion or war with the will of Allah. It is incumbent on dar al-Islam to make war upon dar al-harb (non-Muslim governments) until such time that all nations submit to the will of Allah and accept Sharia law.

Islam also believes the premise that dying while waging jihad is the purest of accomplishments... "But nothing compares to the honor of shahadah kubra (the supreme martyrdom) or the reward that is waiting for the Mujahideen." (That's a quote from Al-Banna.)

Employment Opportunities:

It was not unusual for civilians to be routinely slaughtered by the Japanese Imperial Army, as well as taken as forced labor for war projects. (Thai Burma Railway used civilians taken from Indonesia as well as Malaya and other neighboring SE Asian countries, as well as POWs.)

Islam has a long history of taking slaves by force, and is currently still perpetrating horrors against indentured servants from other countries, especially in Saudi Arabia. (http://www.bbc.co.uk/news/world-asia-pacific-11795356)

Conclusion:

The punishments meted out to civilians and POWs by the Imperial Japanese Army have been recorded by history as shocking — atrocities that still sicken to this day. The belief in their superiority over all others led to acts of pure evil being perpetrated, for which they were condemned by all western nations.

Why then, does a doctrine that is easily aligned with Bushido still exist? (Bushido already having been condemned as inhuman and vile.) Why is this doctrine still being allowed to infiltrate our daily lives? Why does the media apologize and excuse it? Why do the politicians of the same nations that held war-crime tribunals against the JIA now trip over each other to appease the latest practitioners?

At the end of WWII, a declaration was given to the Japanese to sign...one of the conditions read: "We do not intend that the Japanese shall be enslaved as a race or destroyed as a nation...The Japanese Government shall remove all obstacles to the revival and strengthening of democratic tendencies among the Japanese people. Freedom of speech, of religion, and of thought, as well as respect for the fundamental human rights shall be established."

In other words, "No More Bushido." Why then, can I not say, "No More Islam" without being accused of hate speech?

All of the above was Western Feminista's comment. When I asked her if I could reprint her analysis, she said yes, and then added:

I sat down after watching the mini series "The Pacific" and Googled the JIA and Bushido and just picked out a few bits that struck me as being creepily similar.

I thought it was strange that so many people compare Islam to Nazism (Jew hatred, etc.) — but I haven't heard anyone looking at it from a "religious spiritual" side...everything the JIA did was in the name of the Emperor and the belief that he was a divine being unable to be criticized. (Even Hitler had people who doubted him...but the Emperor didn't.)

My Grandfather was on the Thai Burma railroad, and he always said that theirs was an ideology that encompassed every aspect of their lives, was completely irrational and evil to the core...

18. Become less self-righteous.

When self-righteousness is expressed, it tends to bring forth self-righteousness in the listener. Self-righteousness (also called "holier-than-thou") is a feeling of smug moral superiority derived from a sense that one's beliefs, actions, or affiliations are of greater virtue than those of the average person.

When you know a lot about Islamic doctrine and the person you're talking with doesn't know anything (but thinks he does), self-righteousness is bound to crop up somewhere.

In a conversation, if someone expresses self-righteousness, that look on their face and tone in their voice tends to arouse self-righteousness in you, doesn't it? And of course, any self-righteousness *you* express does the same to any listener who doesn't agree with you.

So ideally, you would not express any self-righteousness at all when you're trying to educate someone about the disturbing nature of Islamic doctrine. The self-righteousness is a barrier to communication, making it almost impossible for your listener to accept what you say.

But Houston, we have a problem. You can't just suppress your own self-righteousness. If you feel self-righteous, it communicates whether you want it to or not. In order to not express self-righteousness, you actually have to *feel* no self-righteousness.

But how can you do that? There is only one way: You must develop genuine empathy for the other person. You cannot see them as an enemy, as an idiot, as a fool, or as anything derogatory. You have to see them as a good human being defending worthy values.

That's a big challenge, psychologically, especially when they are simultaneously ignorant about Islamic doctrine *and* self-righteously thinking they know more than you. But you can do it. You can see them as a good human being defending worthy values. And when you do, your persuasive efficacy will increase.

You were once ignorant about Islam too, and you may also have had a difficult time believing a religion could be so intolerant in its core doctrines. I know I did. I did *not* want to believe it. Most of us felt that way in the beginning. And we felt that way for good reasons. In this culture, we are committed to fairness, to religious freedom, and to protecting the defenseless. These are some of the core values that make our culture worth defending.

You have to see that when a non-Muslim argues against what you're saying and tries to defend Islam, he or she is ultimately motivated by these core values — values that are so instinctive that the impulse to protect them arises automatically and with heroic strength.

Now that you have learned more about Islam, you have not given up those values. You have simply added more information and more distinctions you didn't have before.

You must try to see your interaction through this light. It will give you more empathy and less self-righteousness.

Your empathy will make your conversations much more pleasant and it will greatly improve your ability to educate. This ability to empathize is one of the things that makes a great leader great. And you are now a leader. You are leading people into the warm light of new knowledge, sometimes against their own resistance. That's what leaders do.

You must see yourself as a leader and use empathy the way other great leaders have done.

To see a good example, watch the movie *Invictus* or read *Mandela's Way* or *Long Walk to Freedom*. Empathy is what made Nelson Mandela a great leader. His goals were against what people naturally wanted to do, especially people who were on his side. But he was able to see the world from his opponents' side, and was able to bring many of them to his side. That's what a leader does.

If you want to increase your ability to educate people about Islam, you will cultivate a heartfelt, sincere, passionate *empathy* for your listener, and this will reduce or even eliminate self-righteousness as a barrier in your conversations.

19. Respond to resistance by asking a simple question.

When you share something about Islamic texts with a non-Muslim and encounter resistance, respond with something like this: "Well, tell me what you've learned about Islamic doctrine so far. Let's start there." Ask the question in a casual, relaxed, easygoing, not-in-the-slightest-bit-defensive way.

Practice asking that question when you are alone, so you can deliver it perfectly and with just the right tone.

After you ask the question, listen. Let the person speak until they're done.

When they finish, tell them what you've found out. Take something specific, and say, "I used to think exactly the same thing until I finally went to the source and read the Koran. And what I found out really surprised me..."

A back-and-forth argument usually doesn't change anyone's mind, and tends to create negative feelings. But the kind of conversation you get with the approach above has a chance of making your listener *consider* what you have to say, which could lead to them changing their mind eventually.

20. Still More on Talking About Islam by Talking About Scientology.

Because Scientology is a new religion and doesn't have a lot of followers, most people have no aversion to learning anything interesting about it.

If you tell a friend something about Scientology and they have no problem with it, and then you say the same thing about Islam and they want you to stop talking about it, you're in a good position to open their minds about Islam. The double standard will be obvious. This can help you sweep aside their unjustifiable antagonism toward learning about Islam. Make the point that we should be free to criticize religious doctrines in a free country.

Along those lines, a very long article in *The New Yorker* is an investigative report on the current state of Scientology, and below I'll quote a few things from the article.

The title of the article is "The Apostate." It's about a famous man who left Scientology (and the stir his exodus caused among Scientologists). The quotes below are things about Scientology that are similar to Islam but unlike any other religion I know about.

The Koran is very clear about the strictness of Islamic teachings, for example. The teachings are perfect as they are. They're not to be altered. There is no "picking and choosing" passages you like or agree with. Islam is Islam, and it is strictly forbidden to ignore or change any part of the teachings.

Along those lines, here is a quote from Tommy Davis, the chief spokesperson for the Church of Scientology International:

> "Mr. Hubbard's material must be and is applied precisely as written. It's never altered. It's never changed. And there probably is no more heretical or more horrific transgression that you could have in the Scientology religion than to alter the technology." (Scientologists consider the teachings of L. Ron Hubbard, the founder, to largely consist of "spiritual technology" — specific methods and "drills" to achieve specific spiritual results.)

Many Islamic organizations use the courts to harass people, and they use organized political and legal actions to intimidate people into doing what they want (apologizing, retracting public statements, keeping silent, firing an employee, etc.). Here's a quote from the article about Scientology. Notice any similarities?

> "The Church of Scientology had recently gained tax-exempt status as a religious institution, making donations, as well as the cost of auditing (a form of 'spiritual coun-

seling'), tax-deductible. (Church members had lodged more than two thousand lawsuits against the Internal Revenue Service, ensnaring the agency in litigation. As part of the settlement, the church agreed to drop its legal campaign.)"

Another thing that becomes very clear in the article is that the spokesperson, Tommy Davis, is lying to protect Scientology, and Scientology's teachings explicitly make clear that lying for the cause of Scientology is completely acceptable. Islam does something similar. Known as the practice of taqiyya, Muslims are given explicit permission in Islamic teachings to lie to non-Muslims if it serves the goals of Islam.

Another similarity is that becoming an apostate is very bad in both Islam and Scientology. Very *very* bad. They both consider it a kind of treason. Leaving the religion is considered a very serious offense. In Islamic law, the punishment is death.

In Scientology jargon, someone who leaves the church has "blown." Apostates are considered "fair game" in Scientology, meaning they can be tricked, lied to, sued, and harassed, as I mentioned earlier. Here is another quote from *The New Yorker* article:

"Whitehill and Valerie Venegas, the lead agent on the case, also interviewed former

Sea Org members in California. (The Sea Org is the headquarters of Scientology worldwide.) One of them was Gary Morehead, who had been the head of security at the Gold Base; he left the church in 1996. (Gold Base is a central Scientology outpost in the desert near Hemet, a town eighty miles southeast of Los Angeles.) In February, 2010, he spoke to Whitehill and told her that he had developed a 'blow drill' to track down Sea Org members who left Gold Base. 'We got wickedly good at it,' he says. In thirteen years, he estimates, he and his security team brought more than a hundred Sea Org members back to the base. When emotional, spiritual, or psychological pressure failed to work, Morehead says, physical force was sometimes used to bring escapees back."

Talk about some of these aspects of Scientology with people you know who are reluctant to listen to information about Islam, and then talk about how similar these aspects are to Islamic doctrine. Don't push too hard; just open up their minds a little. Think small bits and long campaigns.

21. Getting the Information to Slip Right Past Their Defenses.

I was talking to a man the other day who had already told me (months earlier) he doesn't believe the Muslims he knows follow the Islamic teachings I told him about, and he is skeptical of my assertion that the Koran is strewn throughout with messages hateful toward non-Muslims that encourage violence against them. And he feels that our U.S. laws will protect us anyway. I'm telling you this so you understand the mindset of the man I was speaking with.

So the other day, I said, "Remember I was telling you I'm reading a book about L. Ron Hubbard?"

He said, "Yeah, I remember."

"Well I finished it and I'm reading another biography of Hubbard. The guy was amazing in his audacity! Remember the Freedom of Information Act?"

"Yeah," he nodded.

"When it passed, the Scientologists discovered that the U.S. government had lots of information on Hubbard and Scientology, and almost none of it was favorable. So Hubbard decided to infiltrate governmental organizations so they could change or destroy that negative information."

"What do you mean?" my friend asked. I had his attention. "How do you 'infiltrate' the government?"

I liked his interest. I could tell this conversation was going to be instructive. I said, "Hubbard assigned a bunch of loyal Scientologists to get jobs at the IRS and other government offices. And then they proceeded to find government documents on Scientology and either steal them or change them or shred them. Unbelievable! I mean, who even *thinks* of doing something like that?!"

"Yeah, that *is* amazing!" he said. He looked genuinely dumbfounded and appropriately outraged.

Then I dropped a bomb on him. I said, "The Muslim Brotherhood has done the same thing."

"What? What do you mean?" I had taken him by surprise.

"They have infiltrated government organizations," I said matter-of-factly.

"What for? What would they do?" I could tell he had never heard anything like this, and could not imagine what a "real" religion would want to accomplish by infiltrating government offices.

My answer, unfortunately, wasn't as good as I would have hoped. I wished I had been better prepared with examples. But I will be next time.

What would the Muslim Brotherhood want to do in government offices? I answered, "All kinds of things that might help Islam advance in America. I told you the clear goal in Islamic doctrine is an Islamic world, remember? Well, the devoted ones intend to accomplish it. So, for example, one guy fairly high up in the U.S. government was caught

trying to get a known Islamic terrorist organization off the FBI 'watch list.' Others have gotten
jobs at the FBI to instruct FBI agents on how to be
careful not to offend the American Muslim population. Others have gotten jobs as interpreters in
security agencies. And we only know about the
ones who got caught, of course. Nobody knows
how many have already infiltrated without getting
caught."

After that, I said something else interesting I
read about in Hubbard's biography. Sometimes,
you need to just let things sink in and not push too
hard. But some new information got through in
that conversation. It's a beautiful thing when it
happens. Step by step, inch by inch, we are converting unwitting enemies into allies for the cause.

22. Talk About Sociopathy First.

I was listening to *Civilization and Its Enemies* last
night. I read the book years ago and thought it was
so good, I bought the unabridged audio version,
which I've listened to four times now. One of the
insights from the book that has finally overridden
the last residue of my youthful idealism is this: It is
a fact of life — a hard, unchangeable fact, like New-
ton's law of universal gravitation — that if someone is willing to risk their life to take something of
yours, you will have to be willing to risk your life
to keep it, or you will probably lose it.

This applies at a personal level and at a national level too.

The author, Lee Harris, was describing what happened after World War One. "The Great War" was so horrible, people would try *anything* to prevent it from happening again. They wanted conflicts between all countries to be handled *civilly* — without bloodshed.

But you will find a Catch-22 embedded in that thinking: The more civilized people get, the more of an opportunity it presents for someone who is not civilized.

Apparently there's a famous example of civility often recounted in books on etiquette that epitomizes the essence of civility and good manners. The late Shah of Iran was sitting at a table with the Queen of England and many other guests. A bowl of rose water was presented to each guest so they could wash their fingers.

The Shah had apparently never been presented with a "finger bowl" and took it for a bowl of soup, so he picked up the bowl and started to sip it. Without hesitating, the Queen picked up her bowl and started to sip it, and everyone else at the table followed her example. Why?

A principle of civilized company — the prime principle of etiquette — is that you don't *ever* make someone feel they've done something wrong. You never make someone feel embarrassed or offended. You *never* let them think that they are not civilized.

But what if they really *aren't* civilized? The rules of etiquette assume the other person cares as much about courteous relations as you do. *But what if they don't?*

I want you to try something: Google "sociopath" and read about the strange and frightening phenomenon of sociopaths who live among us, not as serial killers, but as ordinary-appearing people who heartlessly use, manipulate, and take advantage of people without the slightest twinge of remorse or regret — and all the while, fooling their victims by imitating human empathy, deliberately giving the false impression they have normal human feelings (because people are easier to manipulate if they think they're dealing with someone with normal human feelings).

One of the articles has a "comments page" and a huge number of people have written their stories — painful, heartbreaking stories of being married to a sociopath, for example. And after 25 years of a nightmarish existence, they finally found out such a thing as sociopathy exists! They never knew it and tried their best to explain their husband's lying, cheating, remorseless behavior in some other way, like blaming themselves, or trying to help the husband "work through" his childhood issues.

And the sociopath, of course, goes along with all this nonsense because it means he can keep getting away with his lying, cheating, remorseless manipulations.

But sociopathy isn't the result of a hard up-bringing; it isn't the result of an "anger issue" or a lack of opportunity, or anything else. It is the result of being *born* as a sociopath — a person who has no capacity for human empathy, no guilt, and no feeling of sympathy for others.

And no amount of any kind of therapy can help a sociopath become less sociopathic. As a matter of fact, those who get therapy become even *more* effectively sociopathic because in therapy they learn how to better manipulate people — they learn what excuses people will buy, and they learn how to convey authentic-looking emotions better. They learn more about people, and it helps them be more successful at fooling non-sociopaths.

Now, a wife who doesn't know such a thing as a sociopath exists explains her sociopathic husband's behavior in some way. She doesn't leave it unexplained. It is almost impossible for a human being to *not* explain something bothering her.

So she explains it. She thinks it's because her husband had a bad childhood, or she herself is not a good enough wife, or whatever. But she comes from the idea that "deep inside, everyone is basically good" and *this assumption* prevents her from grasping the true nature of her husband's character.

She can't conceive of the real explanation, and *because* she can't, she becomes an ongoing victim.

I think the same is true on a global scale dealing with any group or country that is willing to be ruthless.

If you have ten countries and they all agree to be civil to each other and work out their differences in a civilized manner and to forgo using violence to solve their differences, they will all get along great. But they will also have created an ideal environment to exploit for someone who is willing to use violence to get their way. In fact, the more civilized those ten countries become, the more vulnerable they will be to exploitation by an uncivilized enemy. The more the ten countries disarm themselves, the more ripe they will be for the picking.

It is just a fact of life you can't get around.

I've been thinking long and hard about what it is that prevents people from accepting simple facts about Islamic doctrine. And I think I've actually finally struck bedrock. This is it. Just like the sociopath's wife who doesn't understand that sociopaths exist (and that her husband is one), our friends and family members don't understand that some *ideologies* are sociopathic, some *cultures* can be sociopathic, some *religious doctrines* can be sociopathic, and this ignorance keeps them vulnerable to exploitation and manipulation, and ultimately to subjugation.

If you don't personally think it's possible for someone to just be born bad, then you can't conceive of the existence of a born sociopath. And if you can't understand that a person can be born a sociopath, then maybe you can't conceive of the possibility that a *religion* could be started by a sociopath and could create an exploitative, violent religious doctrine, creating a global movement of dominance-oriented political action embedded in the trappings of religion.

And the more *firmly* people don't want to believe such a thing exists, the more *easily* they are defeated and subjugated by those who are following this creed. The more civilized people get, the more *unwilling they are* to make anyone feel wrong, the more easily they are bowled over and manipulated by those who are willing to exploit their ignorance and civility.

Knowledge of sociopathy is the antidote to all our difficulties.

Okay, I'm probably overstating my case. But if people understood that sociopaths exist, and if they understood that a sociopath can't be changed or improved, and if they understood that some people are just born that way, then they could understand that not everyone is a good person "deep down" and then they could understand it's possible for a religion to be started by a sociopath, by someone who only wanted to exploit the features of a religion. And if they could get *that*, they might be able to listen to a description of such a "religion."

And if they could get *that*, they might actually be willing to defend themselves against it.

Once those spouses of sociopaths *finally* realize that sociopathy exists, once they finally identify their spouse as a sociopath, they usually have no problem at all ending the relationship and stopping their own victimization. Their realization and reversal is often sudden and complete.

I think if these people to whom we've been trying to get through finally realized sociopaths exist, through this chain of realizations, they could ultimately stop being the naïve, exploited victims of orthodox Islam's ruthless aggression.

23. Use the Principle of Commitment and Consistency.

This is one of the six "weapons of influence" from the book, *Influence: The Psychology of Persuasion*. The principle says that once you have committed yourself to something, you tend to remain consistent. That is, you become resistant to changing your mind about what you believe (once you have expressed some commitment to it).

And the more you have done to express your commitment, and the more public you have made your commitment, the more resistant you are to changing your mind about it.

For example, in one experiment, researchers went around in a neighborhood and asked people if they would be willing to put a three-inch square sign in their window that said "Be a safe driver."

Two weeks later, a different volunteer went door to door through the same neighborhood and asked for something outrageous: "Would you be willing to put a billboard on your lawn supporting driver safety?"

Those who had earlier agreed to the little sign were *much* more likely to say yes to the billboard than people who had refused the little sign. And almost everyone who they asked to put the billboard on their front lawn (who had *not* been asked to display the little sign) refused.

In other words, once someone had committed themselves a little bit to the cause by putting the small sign in their window, *they were more committed to the cause.* They were more willing to do something about it. This is the principle of commitment and consistency.

The author, Robert Cialdini, defined the principle this way:

> "It is, quite simply, our nearly obsessive desire to be (and to appear) consistent with what we have already done. Once we have made a choice or taken a stand, we will encounter personal and interpersonal pressures to behave consistently with that commitment. Those pressures will cause us to respond in ways that justify our earlier decision."

So when you can get someone to sign a petition to stop Saudis from teaching hatred in American schools or to stop imams from preaching jihad in American mosques, the person who signs it commits herself a little to the cause.

It is a small act. It only takes a few moments, and it may hardly seem worth doing. But signing a petition makes her more committed to the cause in general. She may begin to think of herself as an advocate for the cause. She will be more likely to commit to something bigger for the cause in the future when an opportunity arises.

Use this principle to get people on our side. Think of a very small thing you can get people to do that supports the counterjihad cause.

24. Use the Principle of Social Proof.

"Social proof" is another of the six "weapons of influence" from the book, *Influence*. When people are uncertain about how to respond, the principle of "social proof" says that people will usually look around and see what others are doing and do the same.

If you see two people have signed a petition, statistically, you will be less willing to sign it than if you see a million people have already signed it — especially if you aren't sure of the merits of the proposition.

If you saw a single protester on the street, would you pay much attention to him? But what if both sides of the street were filled with protesters? Wouldn't it make you curious about what they were protesting? This is the principle of social proof.

A just read a good example of social proof in the book, *The New Concise History of the Crusades*. The crusaders were trying to capture the great walled city of Constantinople, but they were out-numbered and the city was well defended.

But by luck, the crusaders made a hole in a back gate to the city, and *one* crusader climbed through the hole to find himself face-to-face with several enemy soldiers.

The lone crusader boldly drew his sword and ran toward the group of enemy soldiers.

For some unknown reason, they turned and ran!

Other soldiers inside the walled city saw their fellow soldiers fleeing from something (they knew not what), and they abandoned their posts and fled too. This panic spread throughout the city.

Amazingly, the crusaders who came through the hole simply walked over and opened the city gates. There were no guards left to stop them. They had all fled.

They easily captured the city — one of the largest and most well-built walled cities in the world at the time. How? Because of the principle of social proof.

Once a few soldiers were seen fleeing, other soldiers didn't know what to do. So they did what others were doing, and the more people who did it, the more it seemed like the thing to do.

Social proof is a powerful principle of influence. We can use this principle in many ways to help defeat the third jihad. For example, when you find a good petition, you can encourage your friends to sign it.

They will see that many other people have felt it was worthy of signing, and that will help them accept the information.

Because of the principle of social proof, that information will be considered more valid. Without any pressure from anyone else, this seedling of validity can evolve into their personal belief.

You can use this principle in personal conversations, too. Think about it for a moment — are you likely to listen to someone who seems to be the only one who thinks that way? Or would you be more open to hearing what millions of people believe?

We need to think about this when we're telling people about Islam. When you talk to people and you imply that "nobody knows this," or that all the mainstream media is crazy, or in any way im-ply that you are the only one who knows "The Truth," you automatically prevent people from listening. Their guard goes up. You've made the social proof principle work *against* you.

Instead, you need to let your listener know that a lot of people think this way. If you can add authority to these other people, so much the better (authority is another one of the six principles of influence).

Let your listener know movies have been made about it, hundreds of books have been written about it, and millions of people are trying to do something about it around the world. Tell them about the successful anti-Sharia legislation being passed by many state legislatures. Tell them about France banning burkas and Switzerland banning minarets. Let them fully understand that this issue is not just the obsession of a few isolated wingnuts. It is a global concern, and serious, well-respected people are trying to do something about it.

This social proof will give weight to what you say and will help awaken people to the situation, and that's what we need right now more than anything.

Conclusion

Let's not get stuck answering argument for argument in one-on-one debates. Presenting a logical, factual argument to answer an argument is a relatively weak tool because the other side of the debate often uses it equally well.

We have more effective tools we can add to our efforts, and we should learn to use them to our advantage. Failure is not an option. We *must* open the minds of our fellow non-Muslims and we must do it soon.

HOW TO RESIST ISLAMIC ENCROACHMENT AND STILL BE HAPPY

IN A SCENE from the movie, *Armageddon*, a young couple is on a picnic, just being with each other and feeling in love, but with a tinge of sadness. He has to leave the next day, and there's a chance he won't survive the mission. It's getting dark. This may be their last few moments alone together. And if the mission fails, the entire human species will be extinguished.

She said, "Do you think there are others in the world doing just what we're doing right now?"

He said, "I hope so; otherwise, what are we trying to save?"

In the counterjihad movement, we know what we are trying to save, don't we? We're trying to save the Western world — freedom of speech, freedom of religion, human rights, women's rights, etc. Why? Because this culture of freedom is the best system ever invented to allow people full self-expression, dignity, individuality, creativity, and happiness. It's worth protecting. It's worth defending. But do we have to be miserable to do it?

Each of us discovered the ugly truth about Islamic doctrine, and each of us feels motivated to help others learn about the basic elements of Islam, and most of us have run face-first into a wall of anger and resistance and argument and judgment and self-righteousness, and our desire to simply help educate our fellow non-Muslims has become a stressful, upsetting, arduous *chore*.

Many drop out of the counterjihad movement because of the stress. They've lost friends. They've alienated relatives. Their life has become no fun. They've lost their happiness.

So they drop out. They burn out. They stop talking about it. The whole exercise seems futile, upsetting, and unbearably frustrating. They think to themselves, "It's going to take a nuclear weapon going off in downtown Chicago before these idiots will wake up." And they give up the fight and leave it to fate.

We can't afford to lose these people. We need to not only *educate* our fellow non-Muslims, but we need also to keep the educated ones *in the fight with us*. We need to try to prevent them from burning out. That means we need to make sure *fighting the good fight* doesn't make us so miserable.

Another good reason to focus some attention on this issue about being upset is that (as every sales organization has discovered) people who are unhappy are not good at influencing others. Most people are repelled by unhappy, angry, frustrated, depressed people. Nobody wants to listen to someone like that. People don't want to be influenced by someone like that. People don't want to *become* someone like that.

So how can we remain in the counterjihad and still be happy? As silly as it may sound, this is an important question.

We have one thing working in our favor already: Having a meaningful purpose can contribute greatly to a feeling of happiness and fulfillment. And if there is one thing we all share in the counterjihad movement, it is a meaningful feeling of purpose. This is often ruined, however, by living in a permanent state of upset, anger, and frustration.

How can we keep the positive feeling of a fulfilling purposefulness while reducing the negative, stressful emotions? If we can solve that problem, fewer of us would drop out of the fight, and our effectiveness would increase.

I don't think there is a single answer to this question. But we have many things we can do to reduce the stressfulness of our purpose and allow us to feel happier while still being dedicated citizen warriors. For example:

Collect and associate with allies. Stay in communication with others in the counterjihad movement. This lowers the stressful feeling of being an isolated outcast. Find like-minded people on Facebook. Join *ACT! for America* and attend their local meetings. Knowing you have people on your side, knowing you're not alone, reduces stress.

Improve your effectiveness. Add new skills to your persuasion repertoire. Add new approaches. Success is uplifting. Failure is frustrating and demoralizing. So the better you get at reaching the people you're trying to reach — the better you become at making your message penetrate and have an *impact* — the less stressful the process is.

Use a stress-reduction technique. An example of a stress-reduction technique is Progressive Relaxation. There are many different ways to directly reduce stress. Find one that works for you and do it when you feel too stressed out. It can make a huge difference to your feeling of well-being and happiness. It's healthy too.

Connect with people you love. Connecting produces oxytocin, an anti-stress hormone that researchers believe is the antidote or counterbalance to stress hormones. One hormone (adrenaline) is for revving up your system to deal with threats; the other hormone (oxytocin) is for calming you, rejuvenating you, and healing. Make sure you get enough oxytocin to stay in balance.

Avoid talking about or reading about Islam an hour before bedtime. This habit has helped me a lot. It makes my sleep more restful. Try it and see if it works the same for you.

Use the cognitive self-therapy process occasionally to clear your mind. It can greatly reduce your feelings of stress and reveal ways to think differently that can prevent stress in the future. The cognitive self-therapy process is this: When you are upset, write down your thoughts. Now go back through what you've written and try to find mistakes in the way you're thinking. Look up David Burns' ten "cognitive distortions" online. It is a list of the ten most common mistakes people make in their thinking (like overgeneralization or the fortune-telling error). When you realize you have made a mistake in your pessimistic, angry, frustrated thoughts, just the realization that your thought is mistaken can often immediately relieve your stress.

Don't try to do everything. Focus on the one aspect of the purpose that interests you most and the one you're most motivated to do. Relax by reminding yourself that there are many of us with you in this fight, and we each have our own specialties and inclinations, and just take a leap of faith and trust that all of it will be done. You can focus on the one thing you're most compelled to do and let the rest go. Let others do what they do, and you do what you do.

Don't watch much mainstream news. Try not to overdo it on the news, period. Especially *watching* news; it is stressful and can be demoralizing. When mainstream news talks about Islam, the amount of distortion can be downright maddening. Take it in small doses.

Do less of the actual persuasion yourself and let DVDs, books, and articles do some of the work for you. Many people will automatically discount what you say about Islam, no matter how much you know, because they do not consider you to be an authority. This can be frustrating and stressful.

But when they watch a DVD showing interviewed experts, they might be more inclined to accept the information. Not only that, but a 90-minute DVD can deliver a *lot* of information, saving you time and trouble.

Focus on persuading people to watch a DVD rather than focusing on persuading them to listen to you about Islam. It's a more efficient use of your time.

Do your best to see things from the other side's point of view. We often get into a right-wrong, us-versus-them, all-or-nothing position, and part of the reason this is stressful is that the world is not as black-and-white as this oppositional stance tries to make it. The other side of this worldwide debate has some legitimate points, and it eases a lot of stress (and makes your arguments more persuasive) to understand those legitimate points and to graciously concede them. I often recommend the book, *The Righteous Mind* by Jonathan Haidt to help you understand the other side better.

Be committed to perpetual learning. Every time something stresses you out, take the time to improve yourself. What can you do *differently* next time that will make it less stressful? The process of learning and growing itself can give you a lift and reduce stress.

Stay healthy. Exercise, eat healthy food, and get enough sleep. These basic things have a big impact on your general feeling of well-being and make you feel less stressed. And when you're feeling better, you are better able to talk to people without contention. If you won't take good care of yourself for selfish reasons, do it for the cause. We need you to feel good as much as you can. You are a far more effective citizen warrior when you feel good.

THE ACHILLES' HEEL OF THE WEST

ACHILLES WAS INVINCIBLE, so the story goes. He was strong and lightning fast, and in every battle he was undefeatable. But when he was shot with an arrow through the back of his heel, he was momentarily disabled, and that gave his enemies enough time to finish him off.

The West seems invincible too. We have superior technology and war-making know-how. We seem undefeatable. But we have a weakness which you already know about. In North America it's "white guilt." In Europe it is "post-colonial guilt."

But this guilt is founded on a mistake that we should all easily see: overgeneralization. If we looked at our guilt from another angle, most of us could clearly recognize the error.

If someone said, for example, "All Muslims should die because of what they did to us on 9/11," almost everyone could see something wrong with the statement. Not all Muslims were involved in bringing down the Twin Towers. Some Muslims hadn't even been born yet. So it would be a moral travesty to punish all Muslims for what some Muslims did.

Let's look at it from another angle. Let's say an African-American kills a European-American in a robbery. Should *all* African-Americans be punished for this? Do you think African-Americans should feel guilty about it? Of course not. Just because someone is a member of your race or religion does *not* mean you're *responsible* for what they do. They are individual human beings, and they choose their own destiny.

All African-Americans should not be held responsible for what any individual African-American does. We can easily see this.

And yet what is white guilt? For a "white" person, it says "because some people in the past had a similar genetic background as yours, and because they did some terrible things to people of dissimilar genetic background (Native Americans or Africans, for example), then *you* should feel guilty about it, and feel responsible for it, and people of your genetic background should do something to make amends for it."

Nobody says this explicitly, but it is an unspoken basic assumption in the hearts of a large percentage of people of European descent. It is a presupposition so widespread, it is almost never spoken aloud, and yet it underlies much of what is spoken and done.

This guilt is a major weakness of the West, and orthodox Muslims are aggressively exploiting it.

As long as we are paralyzed by this guilt-arrow through our heel, orthodox Muslims have the upper hand. We are vulnerable.

Many of us have familiarized ourselves with Islamic doctrine, and we seek to educate our fellow non-Muslims about the information, and we seek to propose solutions to the problem, but we are often labeled as "racists." It's an oxymoron. It does not make any sense. It's crazy. But it is effectively making many people in prominent places — politicians and many news commentators, for example — back off from saying anything honest about the tenets of Islam.

Very few people have examined this underlying guilt clearly enough to recognize the unarticulated, mistaken assumption it's based on, so any public accusation of racism can be devastating to a person's career.

A sizable portion of the population is motivated to bend over backwards for Muslims because of an undiscerning guilt — a guilt that stems from a feeling that "we" have harmed people of other religions and races and that we can (and should) make it up to the "oppressed" and "downtrodden" underdogs of the world.

I heard a 19 year-old freshman in college talking the other day about his class in early American history. He was upset about all the terrible things "we" did to the Native Americans. He clearly felt appalled and guilty about it. I asked him, "Have you ever done anything bad to a Native American person?"

"No," he said, "but white people did."

"Are you somehow responsible for what other white people did?" I asked.

He seemed confused. He had completely accepted the point of view of his teacher and textbook (it's the standard position of many teachers and textbook authors that "we" should feel guilty for what "we" did).

I asked him, "If you were transported back to those times, would you have done anything bad to the Native Americans?"

He said, "I don't think so."

I said, "Were any of your ancestors living in America at that time?"

"I don't know."

"So let me get this straight," I said, because I can't seem to leave well enough alone sometimes, "your ancestors may have still been living over in Europe and had nothing to do with what other Europeans were doing to the Native Americans, and even if your ancestors *were* living in America at the time, you really are not responsible for what your great, great, great grandparents did anyway, are you? I mean, do you feel you should serve jail time for a murder your great, great, great, grandfather committed? And yet here you are feeling guilty for something you would never do and have never done? Doesn't that seem kind of crazy?"

People accept this point of view — this white guilt or post-colonial guilt — and they teach their children the same guilt. *And it has consequences.*

When the Muslim Students Association wants to create their own prayer room just for Muslims on a college campus, they make their appeal to administrators who have a deep-seated, well-ingrained white guilt, and these Muslims *know* the administrators have this guilt, and they press on that sore spot.

It usually doesn't take much before the administrators acquiesce. And now a little Muslim enclave has just been created. A little piece of Sharia law has been implemented (every concession to Islam is an incremental establishment of Sharia law because the only concessions they ask for advance the cause of Islam's prime directive).

And as time goes on, the concession becomes accepted as permanently established because it's "always been there."

Muslims are getting away with this sort of thing all over the free world. In this gradual way, Western culture is giving way to Islamic culture.

What causes Western culture to give way? The main culprits are this white guilt we've been talking about, and survivor guilt, which we'll explore in the chapter after next.

If a student had come in and said, "We are Scientologists and we want our own prayer room," the administrator would have chuckled and wondered how someone could be so stupid as to think they could demand such a thing on a college campus!

Why the different response? White guilt does not apply to Scientology. Or Catholicism. Or Protestantism.

Everywhere orthodox Muslims are pressing for concessions — concessions they would not get if they were Catholics or Scientologists — the white guilt blinders need to be removed so their request can be seen for what it is, and those special privileges and special considerations can then be refused in exactly the same way all the others would be refused, and with no guilt.

"We" don't owe anybody anything because of what "our" ancestors may have done. We have all arrived here now. Let's move forward.

When you're talking to your friends, keep your ears tuned to white guilt. You will often hear it as a presupposition in what they say. *Point it out* when you hear it. Shine some light on it. Ask them if they feel guilty. Ask them if they feel responsible for what other Americans or Europeans or Caucasians have done in the past. And make it clear to them that this is the same mistake — this is the identical mistake — that racists make when they say some derisive comment about a race.

Your friend's guilt arises from an overgeneralization.

The more people we can get to grasp this principle, the more *effectively* orthodox Muslims will be thwarted in their efforts to gain concessions. Right now the free world is unwittingly, continually, and even enthusiastically yielding to this relentless Muslim pressure. Let's put a stop to it every place we can.

THE TERRIFYING BRILLIANCE
OF ISLAM

IF YOU WANTED to deliberately design a collection of ideas with the purpose of making an idea-collection that might eventually out-compete every other idea-collection (religion or political system) on earth, you would be hard-pressed to do better than Islam.

Let's look at some of the individual ideas within the collection, keeping in mind that many of the ideas enhance each other. In other words, adding one idea to the others can make the whole collection more effective because some ideas can work together synergistically.

Below are some of the key components of the package of ideas (or bundle of beliefs) known as Islam:

1. A standardized version of the idea-collection is written down. This is something basic to several religions and isn't an Islamic invention, but it is an important factor in the success of Islam.

Something only transmitted orally can change over time, but something printed will be *identical* a thousand years from now, and with printing presses, can be reproduced in the *millions*, giving it an enormous advantage in spreading identical copies of the idea-collection.

2. The Koran includes instructions for its own spread. It tells believers they must spread Islam. It is their holy duty to bring Muhammad's warnings and Islamic law to every corner of the world.

3. The idea-collection includes instructions for its own preservation, protection, and replication fidelity. The Koran — the most important of the Islamic holy books — directly tells its followers that they can never change or modify or "modernize" any of the teachings within the idea-collection. It is perfect *as it is.* It is a capital sin to try to alter or ignore any of it. This idea ensures the preservation of the whole collection.

These first three ideas are pretty standard for several successful religions. But now it gets interesting...

4. Islamic texts command Muslim followers to create a government that supports Islamic norms. This may be one of the most ingenious ideas in the whole collection. Islam is the only religion that uses this. Other groups of religious *people* have had political aspirations, but no other major religious group orders its followers — as a religious duty — to create a government that follows its own system of law.

Islam has a system of law, called *Sharia*, and all Muslims are *morally obligated* to continually strive to make their government — wherever they are — follow the laws of Allah.

Because of some of the other ideas added to Islam, you will see that this political addition to the idea-collection has had significant consequences.

5. Permission to spread the religion using war. This is another smart innovation. Although some other religions have obviously spread themselves using force, they had very little justification from their own religious doctrines to do so.

That is not the case with Islam. Expanding by conquest is encouraged by the idea-collection.

Islamic teachings present it this way: The poor non-Muslims not living in an Islamic state need to be saved from the sin of following laws other than Allah's. If they won't voluntarily adopt Sharia law, then it is the duty of Muslim warriors to insist, on the principle that non-Muslims don't know what's good for them. So, like a parent enforcing a bedtime on their child, orthodox Muslims can (and do) feel quite comfortable *forcing* Islamic law on non-Muslims.

According to Islamic doctrine, the world cannot ever be at peace until everyone on earth has been subjugated under the laws of Allah. That's why even Islamic terrorists doing horrific deeds in the name of Islam can sincerely say, "Islam is a religion of peace."

Muhammad's own experience showed the example. At first, Muhammad tried to spread his new religion by peaceful means. After thirteen years he had a paltry 150 converts.

But then he changed tactics and started using warfare, intimidation, violence, slaughter, executions and assassination, and within ten years he converted tens of thousands, and after he died, his followers used the same tactics and converted *millions*. It is now well over a *billion*.

Permission to use warfare to extend Islam's domain combines synergistically and powerfully with the instruction to create an Islamic state with Islamic laws.

So Islam spread quickly as Muslim armies got bigger. They conquered and set up Islamic states, and most of those lands are still, to this day, Muslim states. The laws within an Islamic state make Islam very difficult to dislodge.

This is one of the most effective methods ever invented for getting an idea-collection into huge numbers of minds. It's a method of control and indoctrination similar to those used successfully in communist and totalitarian states.

But as you'll discover below, Islamic principles make unique use of the power of the law to enforce complete conversion to the religion.

6. Lands must be conquered. And any land that Islam has lost must be *reconquered*, like Spain and Israel, for example. The Islamic empire must continually expand. Since the goal is universal Sharia law, Islamic contraction is bad; Islamic expansion is good.

So if a land was once Islamic and now it is not, that's *contraction*, and must be reversed.

According to Islamic teachings, the earth is Allah's. If there are parts of the earth not following Islamic law, it is the duty of the faithful to gain control of that land and establish Sharia. It is a sin to voluntarily let it be.

7. The idea-collection provides for a maximum number of soldiers of Allah by allowing polygamy. A Muslim man can marry up to four wives, and he can have sex with as many slave girls as he can capture, and *all* his offspring are automatically Muslim because the father is a Muslim.

The Koran especially encourages men to marry *widows*. This is an important idea to add if you are going to be losing a lot of soldiers in war. You need some way of replenishing your army. Otherwise the idea-collection could die out from a lack of offspring.

8. It is a punishable offense to criticize Islam. You can see why this one is a good supporting idea for the collection. It helps suppress any ideas that would reduce the authority of Islamic ideas. This principle, like many of the others, is good for the idea-collection, but bad for the human beings who hold the belief. This one limits freedom of speech and freedom of thought.

This idea is expressed throughout Islamic doctrine, and Muhammad set a fierce example of punishing people who criticized him or Islam. The punishment was often death.

9. You can't leave Islam once you're in. This is an interesting one. It is actually *illegal* in Islamic states to convert out of Islam. This is a critical part of Sharia law. Someone who has rejected Islam but who was once a Muslim is an "apostate." This is a crime and a sin, and the punishment for it is death (and eternal damnation in hell thereafter).

Obviously, you can see why this idea has been included in the collection, but this one has actually caused Islam a problem because those who are following Islam to the letter consider more "moderate" Muslims (those who want to ignore or alter the more violent or intolerant passages of the Koran) to be *apostates.*

Since the punishment for apostates is death, fundamentalist Muslims are fighting modernizing Muslims all over the world, and keeping many rebellious, modernizing Muslims from speaking up for fear of violence.

When a group of Muslims decides that maybe Islam should be updated for the 21st century and maybe women should have more rights or maybe the government should be more democratic or at least less dictatorial, the devout Muslims call them apostates and repress them, throw them in prison, or even kill them.

The idea-collection of Islam has many elements designed *to protect its own fidelity* (its own consistency — staying true to the unalterable original message). This is not good for the organisms (the Muslim human beings), but it's great for the collection (the religion/ideology/political system).

Along the same lines, in Sharia law it is a punishable offense to try to convert a Muslim to any other religion.

10. Islam must be your first allegiance. This is a great idea to add to the collection *if the goal is world domination.* You are a Muslim first, before any allegiance you might give to your family, your tribe, or your country.

This causes a unity of people across borders, which allows Islam to grow bigger than *any other entity.* The "Nation of Islam" can grow bigger than any country, no matter how large (which gives the group a massive numerical advantage).

11. You must read the Koran in Arabic. This rule unites believers by language, and language can be a very potent unifying phenomenon. For added incentive to learn Arabic, another idea in the collection says you can't go to Paradise unless you *pray* in Arabic.

12. To die in jihad is the *only* way to *guarantee* a man's entrance into Paradise. This is an inspired idea for creating the kind of fearless, enthusiastic warriors Islam has historically been known for, especially given the Koran's vivid descriptions of the sensuous delights of Paradise.

A Muslim man has a *chance* of getting to Paradise if he is a good Muslim, but it is not guaranteed.

However, if he dies while fighting for Islam, he is *guaranteed* to get in, and that's the only thing he can do to guarantee it.

13. You must pray five times a day. This is one of the five "pillars" — that is, one of the five central religious practices — of Islam. Within the borders of an Islamic state, it is enforced by law. Every Muslim *must* pray five times a day. The practice helps the idea-collection dominate a Muslim's life, infusing his daily rhythm with Islam.

It would be impossible to forget anything you deliberately do so often. *Five times a day*, every day, a Muslim must bow down and pray to Allah.

Research has shown that the more effort a person expends for a cause, the more he is likely to believe in it, feel committed to it, and find value in it.

So insisting that people pray five times a day is a strategically clever way to eventually make believers out of even those people who became Muslims through coercion.

Islam takes over every aspect of a Muslim's life. Not only are Muslims required to perform the required prayers five times a day, they have to go through a washing ritual beforehand too.

Islamic doctrine dictates the laws, and those laws cover many public and private behaviors. Under enforced Sharia law, it is nearly impossible to be a half-hearted or casual Muslim.

14. Islamic prayers involve moving together in time. When Muslims pray, they all face the same direction, they bow down together, get on their hands and knees, and put their face on the mat, all in unison, and then rise back up. Again and again.

When people move together in time, whether dancing or marching or praying, it creates a physical and emotional bond between them. That's why almost all military training all over the world involves close-order drills (marching in unison), even though it has been a long time since military groups have actually marched into combat.

There is no longer a need for the skill of marching together, but military training retained the practice because it so effectively creates a strong feeling of unity between soldiers.

The same is true of any physical movements people make in unison. So the Muslim method of prayer creates a unifying effect — uniting Muslims everywhere.

15. Women are kept in a thoroughly subordinate position. This idea really helps support other ideas in the collection, particularly numbers five and six. If women had too much influence, they'd try to curb the warfare. Women in general don't like to send their husbands and sons off to war, *especially* when those men are determined to die in battle. But if women have no say, then the rest of the ideas can express themselves without interference. By subordinating women, the idea-collection prevents their effective vote against war, violence, and conquest.

The rules, customs and laws within Islam that keep women subordinate are numerous. For example, she is not allowed to leave her house unless she is accompanied by a male relative. Under Islamic law, a woman is forbidden to be a head of state or a judge. She can only inherit half of what a man can inherit. In court, her testimony is only worth half of a man's. She is not allowed to choose where she will live or who she will marry. She is not allowed to marry a non-Muslim or divorce her husband.

He, however, can divorce her with a wave of his hand. And according to Sharia law, he can (and should) beat her if she disobeys him.

All of these ideas keep her subordinate, which helps the war machine continue unimpeded by domestic resistance.

16. The only way a woman can get into Paradise for certain is if her husband is happy with her when she dies. When I first came across this one, I thought, "Muhammad, you were a crafty one."

This idea obviously helps with the subjugation of women. It motivates her to subjugate *herself*. It provides her with a strong incentive to subordinate her wishes to her husband's, because while she might have a *chance* to get into Paradise if she is a good Muslim, the only way she can *guarantee* she will go to Paradise (and avoid eternal suffering in hell) is *to make sure* her husband is happy with her when she dies.

17. Allah gives himself permission to edit his own work. This is an interesting one. It says in the Koran that if a passage written later contradicts an earlier passage, then the one written later is the better one. The Koran was written in 114 sections (Muhammad's revelations, each written as a *sura* or chapter) over a period of 23 years. The circumstances of Muhammad's life (and the nature of his revelations) changed quite a bit over those eventful 23 years.

One of the ideas in the Koran is: "the Koran is the word of Allah." People had already memorized his earlier revelations, so Muhammad couldn't just change the nature of his revelations. It would look a little strange for the all-knowing, infinitely wise Allah to change something He had already said.

But with this new idea — that later revelations abrogated or overwrote any of the earlier revelations they contradicted — Allah's methods could change as Muhammad found more effective ideas.

As I hope I have already made clear, Muhammad changed tactics mid-career and radically improved his conversion rate.

The peaceful ways were *too slow*. Conversion by conquering and establishing Sharia was much faster and more efficient. What allowed this to happen was the profound shift in the nature of the Koran's revelations.

18. The Koran uses the carrot and stick to reinforce behavior. Throughout the Koran are vivid descriptions of hell, where sinners and non-Muslims will have to drink boiling, stinking water, will be thrown face down into a raging fire, and will be there for eternity, suffering endless torments in agony.

There are also vivid and detailed descriptions of Paradise. In Paradise, it says, believers will wear green silk robes and recline on plush, comfortable couches. Trees will shade them and fruit will dangle nearby. They'll have tasty food and refreshing drinks served in silver goblets.

But to have a chance of making it to Paradise, they must be devout Muslims. To *guarantee* it, men must die in jihad and women must make sure their husbands are happy with them.

19. It provides a huge and inspiring goal. Leaders of countries and companies and religions have all discovered that you can get the most motivation and enthusiasm from your followers if you provide them with an expansive vision — an enormous goal. In the Islamic idea-collection, the goal calls for a continuous effort to expand the domain of Islamic rule until all the world is subject to it.

Many religions have the goal of converting everyone, but Islam has a method available to nobody else: To increase the conversion rate by seizing and converting *governments* to a system of law that strongly encourages conversion.

The Koran says it would be ideal if non-believers accepted Islam and became Muslims without force. But if they refuse, then Muslim believers must fight them and conquer them and save their poor souls by insisting they at least live by the laws of Allah, subject to the onerous dhimmi regulations that make converting to Islam seem like a good idea. Search online for "The Conditions of Omar" to find out more about dhimmi regulations.

This worldwide, historically-significant goal is inspiring to believing Muslims, and it provides a unifying purpose. The mission creates motivated, enthusiastic followers.

20. Non-Muslims must pay a heavy tax. Once Muslims conquer a country and convert the government to Islamic law, Jews and Christians have the choice between becoming Muslims or becoming dhimmis.

Dhimmis are allowed to practice their non-Muslim religion if they pay the jizya (a tax). If they convert to Islam, they no longer have to pay the jizya, so there is a practical incentive to convert.

But another aspect of this makes it a brilliant idea to add to the collection. The tax takes money away from the non-Muslims and their competing idea-collections and gives that money to support Islam. This is pure genius!

The income from these taxes (usually a 25% to 50% income tax) helped fund the Islamic conquests during the first two major jihads.

War is expensive. But Muslims conquered vast lands, most of them already filled with Christians and Jews, many of whom did not convert at first, and their jizya poured huge sums of money into the Islamic war machine.

Eventually, the numbers of Christians and Jews dwindled down as they converted or escaped, until now, in most Islamic countries, Jews and Christians are very small minorities.

The tax-the-non-Muslims idea helps the Islamic idea-collection make more copies of itself by suppressing any competing religious idea-collections and financially supporting Islam. That's really clever.

Several ideas within Sharia law extend this effect. For example, non-Muslims are not allowed to build any new houses of worship. They are not

even allowed to repair any already-existing churches or synagogues. This puts the houses of worship of any competing idea-collection in a state of
permanent decline. Brilliant.

Also, non-Islamic prayers cannot be spoken
within earshot of a Muslim — which prevents Muslims from being "infected" by a competing religion. No public displays of any symbols of another
faith may be shown either.

All of this prevents the spread of any competing religion, and makes competing idea-collections
die out over time. That's why today we have "Muslim countries." Almost every other country in the
world is made up of many different religions. But
the longer a country has been a Muslim country,
the fewer members of any other religion live within its borders.

One added idea makes it that much easier for
Muslims to dominate non-Muslims within an Islamic state: Non-Muslims are not allowed to own
weapons of any kind. To subjugate a people, all
dictatorial rulers in the history of the world have
done the same thing: Disarm the subjugated population. They're much easier to manage, less dangerous, and a lot less capable of overthrowing the
existing government.

**21. A Muslim is forbidden to make friends with
an infidel.** A Muslim is allowed to *pretend* to be a
friend, but in his heart he must never *actually* be a
friend to a non-Muslim. This is one of the best pro-

tections Islam has against Muslims leaving the religion because in every other religion, the most common way a conversion happens is through a friend, of course. Being forbidden to make friends with infidels prevents that from happening.

22. Islamic texts counsel the use of deceit when dealing with infidels.
Muhammad instructed one of his followers to lie if he had to (in order to assassinate one of Muhammad's enemies). This set the precedent. The principle was clear: If it helps Islam, it's okay to deceive non-Muslims.

This principle has served Islam's prime directive very well through history. And it continues to serve that goal today.

Watch the DVD, *Obsession: Radical Islam's War Against the West*, and see footage of Islamic leaders saying one thing in English for the Western press, and saying the complete opposite to their own followers in Arabic a few days later, without any apparent guilt or shame about it.

Deceiving the enemy is always useful in war, and orthodox Islam considers itself at war with the non-Islamic world until the whole world follows Sharia law.

To an orthodox Muslim, all non-Muslims living in non-Islamic states are the enemies of Allah. So deceiving Westerners is totally acceptable. It is *encouraged* if it can increase the spread of Islam.

And so we have the strange phenomenon covered by Steven Emerson in his documentary, *Ter-

rorists Among Us, where organizations in America were ostensibly raising money for orphans, but in actuality giving the money to terrorists. They deceived good-hearted Western infidels into giving money to organizations that were actively *killing* Western infidels.

As Muhammad said, "War is deceit." This idea gives Islam a tremendous advantage over idea-collections that encourage indiscriminate truthfulness.

23. Islam must always be defended. This idea is a primary linchpin that gives justification for war with almost anybody, as you'll see in the idea below. After the enemy is defeated, of course, Muslims are required to establish an Islamic state.

24. Islamic writings teach the use of pretext to start conflicts with non-Muslims. The Koran devotes a lot of time complaining about people who did not support Muhammad when he first started his religion, with Allah often condemning them to torment in hell in the hereafter. The Koran is intensely intolerant of non-Muslims.

Muhammad was rather pushy and insistent with his religion, and when others felt intruded upon and protested, Muhammad decided this meant they were trying to stop Allah's holy prophet from bringing the revealed word of Allah to the world, so he was justified to fight them and destroy them because they were enemies of Allah. This is a demonstration of the principle of *pretext*.

Non-Muslims of the world need urgently to become aware of this principle.

Of all the ideas in the Islamic collection, this is the most dangerous to the West because it so effectively removes our natural self-preserving instincts. The use of pretext tends to make the West defenseless against the Islamic invasion now underway. Orthodox Muslims are *not necessarily* backward people. Many are smart, educated, well-funded, and being used by a wily, cunning idea-collection. The invasion and subversion of the West has already begun, and it is being done so cleverly, most Westerners don't even know it is happening.

The use of pretext means you need only the barest excuse to begin hostilities. It means you're actually *looking* for an excuse, and even trying to provoke others into striking the first blow (thus "starting" the hostilities).

If the only way to get to Paradise is to die while fighting for Islam, you *need* war. And if it is your holy duty to make all governments use Sharia law, you need to conquer those governments. But you don't really want to look like the aggressor. Appearances count. All throughout the Koran, Muhammad tries to justify his aggression as *defending* Islam.

The Koran makes it very clear that followers of Islam should use Muhammad as a model and imitate him. So Muslims the world over try to find or create grievances, so they can get a holy war started, so they can fight and die in Allah's cause and help create a world ruled by Allah's laws.

And because of the rise of multiculturalism in the West (respect for all other cultures), the use of pretext is *very* effective against people who are unfamiliar with Islam.

Many people thought al Qaeda was angry at the West for having troops in Saudi Arabia, for example, and they believed that's why they attacked us on 9/11. That's a classic Mohammedan pretext. They wanted all non-Muslims out of the Middle East. Then they said they would cease hostilities. It is a ridiculous and intolerant goal, and *extremely* unlikely to ever happen, so as far as they are concerned, they are justified to wage a permanent war against the West as they "defend Islam from the Crusaders."

It's surprising that so many Westerners accept this particular pretext because it flies in the face of a fundamental Western principle: Equality. What Osama bin Laden was saying was "infidels are so unsavory, their very presence anywhere within our borders defiles all our holy places." Wow. What does that say about non-Muslims?

Why doesn't this kind of racism or prejudice or infidelphobia (or whatever you want to call it) outrage more Westerners? You'll find out why in the next chapter. But the fact is, it doesn't outrage many Westerners. Instead, some think we ought to pull out of the Middle East so these poor offended

Islamic supremacists aren't so angry with us any more! This is the West's Achilles' heel at work: White guilt. Like I said, the misplaced guilt is a major weakness being constantly exploited. Imagine how outraged people would be at the proposition that we should expel all Muslims from our country because their very presence defiles all our holy places! Why don't Westerners feel offended by the double standard? Because of white guilt.

The principle of pretext means you try to provoke a hostile reaction and then use the hostile reaction as a reason to escalate hostilities. It's the same method schoolyard bullies have used for thousands of years: "What are *you* looking at? You got a problem?! You wanna take it outside, punk?"

25. The explicit use of double standards. Islam has one standard for Muslims, and a *different* standard for non-Muslims, which always gives the advantage to Muslims.

For example, Islam must be spread by its believers, wherever they are. But when other religions try to spread *their* idea-collection, orthodox Muslims see it as *an aggression against Islam* — an act of aggression that must be "defended against." Remember, Islam must *always* be defended.

Another example of how the double standard idea gives Islam an advantage: When Islam is defamed in any way, Muslims violently protest it. Even if the defamation was a mere *cartoon*. During the infamous "cartoon riots" in 2006, a hundred and eighty-seven people were *killed.*

But orthodox Muslims can (and do) openly and shamelessly defame Jews and Christians in Muslim newspapers and television, and they defame any infidel or enemy, as they defame the U.S. today. The Koran itself defames Judaism and Christianity quite harshly. And every other belief system even more harshly.

Here's another example of a double standard: The orthodox Muslims of Saudi Arabia — the center of the Muslim world — are pouring their abundant oil money into building mosques all over the world. But in Saudi Arabia, no non-Muslim religious structures are allowed to be built within the country. None. And orthodox Muslims all over the world protest loudly and sometimes violently when anyone in Europe or America resists the building of more mosques in their countries.

Orthodox Muslims don't see any irony in it. They don't feel strange having such a glaringly blatant double standard. They are, after all, Allah's followers and everyone else is doomed and deluded. Fairness and equality with such unworthy infidels would seem completely out of place to a believing Muslim. A double standard seems appropriate from that perspective.

The double standard principle is a key part of the idea-collection, and it has been a great advantage in the spread of Islam (and the suppression of competing religions).

26. It is forbidden to kill a Muslim (except for a just cause). It is not forbidden to kill an infidel. This causes a bond between Muslims, fear in non-Muslims, and motivation to become Muslim. And this is also another example of an explicit Islamic double standard.

27. If Muslims drift away from Mohammed's teachings, Allah will end the world. That makes converting others and promoting Islam a matter of *survival*. It also motivates Muslims to prevent each other from losing faith.

28. The message in a standard Koran is difficult to decipher. Whether it was done intentionally or not, the Koran's message has been scrambled and in a sense, coded. This discourages almost all non-Muslims and a significant percentage of *Muslims* from understanding it.

In what way is the message scrambled? First, the chapters are published out of order in every standard Koran.

Rather than printing them using the chronological order in which they were revealed, the 114 chapters (suras) of the Koran are arranged using a baffling method: They're in order from the longest chapter to the shortest.

If you were to read a standard Koran straight through like a normal book, you would find the message disjointed. The story jumps back and forth in time and seems contradictory. One very important consequence of this curious disorder is that it hides the clear progression from Muhammad's semi-tolerance of non-Muslims to his violent hatred toward them.

The disorder also prevents the layman from figuring out which passages are abrogated unless they know the chronological order of the Koran.

The second way the Koran has been put into "code" is by putting the key *somewhere else*. Much of the Koran cannot be understood without being familiar with the life of Muhammad (by reading the Sira and the Hadith, the other two primary Islamic texts). These are primarily about Muhammad — what he said and did.

In other words, the Koran — the source book, the single most important source book in Islam — can't be understood without the key, and the key can only be found somewhere else, which is similar to one of the ways a message can be written in code: You put the key to understanding the message somewhere else and do not include it with the message.

This is enough to keep most non-Muslims from understanding the Koran, and also keeps most ordinary Muslims on a need-to-know basis. So the only ones who really know what's going on are the imams and the scholars. They call the shots. Everyone else is in the dark.

If the Koran wasn't put into code deliberately, it has been a tremendously fortuitous accident which has served the goals of Islam very well throughout history.

~~~

WE CAN ADMIRE the brilliance of the Islamic idea-collection in an abstract, intellectual sort of way, but it is terrifyingly *real*. Millions of people try to follow these ideas to the letter. And their belief in the idea-collection is strongly supported by the side-effects of Sharia law. By making the government and laws follow Islamic teachings, the idea-collection applies two powerful principles of influence: social proof, and authority.

Every Muslim must practice the religion in an Islamic state (or they are flogged, taxed, or killed) and no one can criticize it, not through any media, and not even friend-to-friend. The psychological impact of this is enormous. Think about it. A mere three generations later, it would be almost impossible for any Muslim living in an Islamic state to think outside of Islam. The authority of Islam and the social proof would be overwhelming.

Of course, just because I admire the genius of the idea-collection *doesn't* mean I'm in favor of it. As a non-Muslim, I am wholeheartedly against it.

The Islamic idea-collection is formidable. It is a force to be reckoned with and we ignore it at our peril. It has already taken hold of the minds and lives of one and a half billion people, and it is the youngest of the major religions.

And yet, I don't think the situation is hopeless. Because of the internet, many Muslims in Muslim countries find it easier to think outside of Islam. Many "Muslims" now living in Muslim countries feel trapped and would defect from Islam if it were safe to do so.

The first thing we in the multicultural and tolerant West need to do is help each other become aware of the nature of this formidable idea-collection.

We need to help our fellow citizens awaken to the fact that orthodox Muslims will deliberately take advantage of our tolerance and our freedom so as to ultimately eliminate it.

This is an ideological war, so the ideas in the heads of your fellow Westerners make all the difference. And *you* can help turn the tide. Find ways to introduce this information to your fellow non-Muslims.

When enough non-Muslims know about it, Islamic tactics like pretext and deceit will be seen for what they are, and will no longer make us defenseless. When we know more about the founder and the goal of Islam, our collective decisions and actions can effectively thwart their plans. Our grasp of the real situation will bring more rational changes to our laws and policies (such as our current immigration policies).

But to do this kind of inoculation, you have to have a pretty good handle on the Islamic teachings themselves. That will require some study.

I know you have other things to do, and you might not be able to make this a full-time occupation, but I also know how serious this is, so it'll require some sacrifice on your part.

After millions of people have fought against tyranny and died to gain the rights and freedoms we enjoy today, we are now confronted with a pernicious idea-collection hell-bent on taking them away. And the Islamic idea-collection could realistically succeed with terrifying brilliance.

Take action today. Learn about Islam. With every new understanding you have, and with every new certainty and clarity you gain, you will feel bolder in speaking up, and speaking up is the first thing we must do to win.

SHOULD WE FEEL ANGER
AT THOSE STILL UNACQUAINTED
WITH ISLAM?

In correspondence with a reader, I wrote: "Over the years, we've had discussions on various things on Citizen Warrior, trying to figure out how to speak about the problem of Islam. One of the things we've talked about is what to call non-Muslims who think Islam is a religion of peace. We had a lively discussion about it here." And I gave him the link to the article. Here is his response:

> What to call Non-Muslims who think Islam is a Religion of Peace...we could call them: Aloof. Here's an example: "the Aloofs were back at it again. They were talking about how we can all just get along and as I stood there listening to them I realized that these people are just Aloof. They have no desire to save themselves or to fight back, so we must do it for them. The Aloofs venture loudly into the world, sharing their propaganda with the other Non-Muslims

who are quite aware what Islam is all about. But the Aloofs insist that Islam is good...

OR

I would just call those people "Islamic Sympathizers." To be honest, we are facing the prelude to the massive extermination of non-Muslims. So if some of the non-Muslims want to be willingly ignorant and believe that Islam is "Peaceful," it really comes down to responsibility and we need to make them aware of that.

Example: If I was given the chance to warn people about Nazi Germany and tell them how horrific it was going to be, I would call everyone who supported Hitler (supporting Hitler by being ignorant) a Sympathizer.

I conclude then that we need to not mock these "Aloofs," but lay the burden of mature responsibility on them, meaning that being "Aloof" about the most bigoted religion on earth is no longer an option for excuse.

I responded to him with this: Your point of view is fairly common in the counterjihad community and I'm glad you said it because I want to articulate something that has been crystallizing in my mind for quite some time.

Both the words "Aloof" and "Sympathizer" make the person wrong. But many people have benign reasons for believing Islam is not dangerous. Many of the non-Muslims unacquainted with Islam are good people — smart people who care about the world and love their country. Their hearts are in the right place. Not all of them, of course, but certainly many of them. Probably most of the ones we talk to.

They have simply made some assumptions about Islam (and about religions and about human beings) that might normally be reasonable, but they're incorrect when it comes to Islam. They assume because it is a religion with a huge number of adherents, it couldn't possibly be the evil Nazi-like ideology the counterjihadists portray it to be. It *couldn't* be! Right?

And of course, any given person you're talking to probably knows several Muslims who are "nice people." From their point of view, it seems reasonable to conclude that the terrorism going on in the world is caused by a few crazy extremists giving Islam a bad name.

Most people unacquainted with Islam don't know the immense scale and global scope of "terrorist attacks." Most people hear about only a small percentage of the attacks that happen every day in the name of Islam. And besides, "other religions also have bad things in their holy books," and so on. You've heard it all before. Most people would think this naturally (that it must be just a few extremists), as a result of plain old human decency and an acquaintance with other religions like Judaism, Buddhism and Christianity. And then the media and politicians and Islamic "experts" all confirm what we all wish was true. PBS, one of the most trusted media sources in the U.S., has repeatedly reinforced this misleading portrait of Islam.

Probably none of our non-Muslim friends and family are terrorist sympathizers. And if they thought they were really in danger, they might, in fact, have the desire to fight back and save themselves. But they have been persuaded to believe (and they really *want* to believe) that we are not in danger from Islam. I don't think most of them are "willingly ignorant." They have an enormous amount of mainstream, seemingly authoritative evidence from most major information sources to confirm what they hope is true.

The article I mentioned above (that started this conversation) and the ensuing discussion eventually concluded that the best word for non-Muslims who think Islam is a religion of peace is "unacquainted." Your portrayal of those un-acquainted with Islam is negatively judgmental, which is completely understandable because you have obviously tried doing what all of us should be doing: talking with people and telling them what you've learned. And you have no doubt exper-

ienced the particular distaste of listening to someone sarcastically or condescendingly tell you how
wrong you are — knowing that this person actually
knows nothing about Islam — while talking to you,
who knows quite a lot about it. It is frustrating.
Infuriating! I get it. I've been there. And so have
most of the people in the counterjihad movement.

But I think it would be helpful to our cause if
we considered it as much our failure as theirs. If
we truly understood their point of view, and if we
had some acquirable skill in influencing people,
that same conversation might well have ended
with a new ally for our cause. Instead, we have
entrenched that person more firmly in their
position. We have failed. That point right there is
where we will win or lose this whole, centuries-
long conflict with Islam — right there in those
"minor" personal conversations where people are
either won over or shoved deeper into their self-
righteous point of view (which unwittingly aids
and abets the enemy).

Any of us can get better at those conversations. We can become more influential. And if we
don't, it is *we* who have been negligent and irresponsible. We should consider ourselves lucky that
we have been raised in a way or exposed to information in a way that we've been able to know the
truth about the problem of Islam. We shouldn't
consider them to be willfully ignorant. There, but
for the luck of the draw, is what you or I would be.

And for many of us in the counterjihad, that is exactly what we were at one point.

I was totally ignorant of Islam until after 9/11. I didn't know anything about it, and never even wondered about it, even though jihad has been going on my entire life. With the Israel/Palestine conflict. With the oil crisis. With the Iranian hostages. With all the hijacked airplanes, attacks on embassies, etc. I never put it together. I never would have guessed that a religion could teach something that would motivate people to do these things. I would have scoffed at the idea if anyone had told me. Not because I was a "sympathizer." Not because I was "willingly" ignorant, although I guess you could call me that, but it seems an unfair indictment. And I *would* fight back to save myself. I just didn't know there was anything to save myself from.

And I think when we talk to someone who is unacquainted with Islam, we would be more effective reaching them and successfully opening their eyes to this horrifying reality (Islamic doctrine) if we didn't think of them as bad people, as irresponsible people, as traitors or sympathizers with enemies, or *anything* derogatory. I think we'd have more luck reaching them if we loved them. Or at least understood their point of view, and understood how they came to those conclusions.

THE KEY TO YOUR LISTENER'S INABILITY TO CONFRONT THE DISTURBING NATURE OF ISLAMIC DOCTRINE

SOMEONE LEFT the comment below and it reminds me of the many similar comments I've gotten over the years, and similar feelings I've had:

> "I am at a complete loss as to why CAIR, ISNA, ICNA, MPAC or this NMLA is even allowed to exist in America! Are some Americans so dumbed down that they don't see the enemy right in front of them? Is this or any political party in government so stupid that they just turn a blind eye to what's happening?"

Can you feel the commenter's exasperation? Have you had this feeling before? We are in a strange situation: The reality of Islam's prime directive is easy to understand and verify, and yet our leaders and our own friends remain in the dark. And when we try to simply share new information we have learned, we find ourselves *unable* to share it — not because we are incapable of articulating it, but because our listeners do backflips trying to invalidate the information. They seem to contort themselves into impossible cognitive pretzels in order to reject simple, factual, easily-verifiable information. It has been baffling to many of us. I know. I have heard from hundreds of our fellow counter-jihadists about this.

And I know how it feels. I sometimes want to write off my fellow non-Muslim friends and family as complete idiots, but I know for a fact many of them are *not* stupid, so what is going on? What could be the cause of their seemingly stubborn stupidity on this subject?

Last night, I was reading Victor Davis Hanson's book, *The Father of Us All*, and he said something I have never thought about before. Namely, that people in the West are acutely aware of the inequalities of the world — we in the West enjoy a material quality of life far better than billions of other people — and for a lot of Westerners, this presents a serious ethical problem.

They feel guilty about it.

They need to assuage their guilt in some way. But here's the key insight I've never thought about before: They need to assuage their guilt in some way *other* than giving up the goodies, because even though they don't like the inequality, they don't want to give up the high quality of life either.

In other words, many people need to have a way to keep enjoying the material riches, but still rectify or expiate the guilt they feel about others being so poor.

The solution many have chosen is to go out of their way to see what's wrong with their own culture, and to give other cultures an undeserved reverence.

A Familiar Solution

This solution is something we are familiar with in our personal relationships. If you are more successful than a friend of yours, for example, one way you can help him feel better and prevent him from resenting you is to point out your own faults. Those who are exceptionally successful often habitually display humility — they make it a point to mention their own personal imperfections. It's the classy thing to do.

The successful person can do this with integrity because everyone has faults, even very competent people, and because every success is partly a result of pure luck — the luck of being born in a free country, the luck of being born with ambition, a high energy, basic intelligence, good health, successful parents, or whatever.

Many people use this stratagem, knowingly or unknowingly, because it helps.

The self-deprecation allows successful people to continue to enjoy the material goodies without feeling too guilty about it around other people, and without making other people feel bad about themselves or resentful of the successful person.

It shows no class to put down the "less fortunate" as lazy, stupid, ignorant, etc. It is vulgar to criticize or humiliate or ridicule the less fortunate, or to brag about how competent and brilliant you are and to imply that's the reason you're successful.

I think the people who will not listen to you about Islam, or who argue in defense of Islam even when they know nothing about it, are doing the same thing on a cultural scale.

In other words, when you, a fellow member of the fortunate class (a Westerner) start bad-mouthing another culture — when you start criticizing Islamic doctrine — you have violated an important code of etiquette. And for them to listen to you and accept what you say is for them to violate it too.

What we're dealing with is a "cultural humility" about Western culture and achievements. You will see people go *out of their way* to point out what is wrong with their own Western culture or their own country or government. They're not casual about this — there is an underlying intensity. They seem very *determined* to criticize their country and culture, and to think of it as wrong and bad.

With this new understanding, it makes sense that it appears to be so deeply felt, and that your listeners seem so irrationally *committed* to stopping you from criticizing Islam and committed to criticizing their own culture. Many people *rely* on this criticism to allow them to enjoy their iPads and nice cars and cell phones without too much guilt.

They feel less guilty because they willingly express a "sufficient" degree of contempt for their own highly successful culture, and they feel (or at least profess) sufficient "admiration" for all other cultures (even if they know nothing about them).

The simple, factual information about Islamic doctrine that you want to share threatens to undermine this whole unformulated creed, which endangers the linchpin of their emotional harmony and ethical congruence. *They can't let it in.*

To let it in would require them to rearrange an important feature of their worldview, their philosophy of life, and their self-image.

This is not a minor matter. This is not a small, inconsequential barrier we can easily sweep aside. It is a major psychological problem that stands in the way of our goal of educating people about Islam.

Understanding what it is and what we're up against is the first step.

Survivor Guilt

We're talking about a psychological problem similar to *survivor guilt*. People who've survived plane crashes (or concentration camps or another event where others have died) sometimes suffer a painful, unrelenting guilt because they survived while others perished. It wasn't fair, and they have a real problem dealing with the unfairness.

Westerners are in a similar position, but on a global scale.

Think about it. We've seen close-up, full-color pictures of our fellow human beings starving in Africa. We have read about people imprisoned in China, tortured in Iran, executed in Saudi Arabia, sold into sex slavery in Cambodia, while we drive to and from our pleasant activities in clean, comfortable cars, casually visit grocery stores overflowing with food, come home to a comfortable shelter with cable television, microwave ovens, high-speed internet, and enjoy an immense degree of personal freedom.

It isn't fair. Yes, we may have worked to earn the money, but if we had been born in Haiti or Somalia or Yemen, our lives would be tragically different, regardless of how hard we worked.

We got lucky and it definitely isn't fair.

At some level, I think most of us feel some kind of guilt about this. I think we should have a name for it. *Born in a Western Country Guilt?* I don't know what to call it, but clearly some of us handle the guilt better than others. How do *you* live with the inequality of the world?

Some people think those of us living in Western countries have created a superior culture, so we *deserve* our wealth.

Some think the European or "white" race is genetically superior.

Some good evidence indicates that from the very beginning of civilizations, the original inception of the inequalities were a result of geography (read about that in a very interesting book entitled, *Guns, Germs, and Steel*).

And some just consider themselves lucky and try to help others when they can.

We have all found a way to live with it, but the people we are having a hard time communicating with about Islam have found a less-than-optimal way of dealing with the inequality. It may be better than the path self-righteous racists use, but it is not ideal (or even adequate) — it is preventing them from confronting and accepting important facts about the real world.

Multiculturalism is one way this guilt manifests itself. Multiculturalism says all cultures are equal. None is better than others.

Moral equivalence is another way the guilt manifests itself. Moral equivalence basically says, "Yes, that other culture does terrible things, but look, we've done terrible things too," so again, we are not better than others.

White Guilt is another. Each of these different manifestations all stem from the same fundamental need to relieve guilt while still being able to enjoy the safety and wealth and comfort of Western culture.

We have a *need*, wrote Hanson, for what he calls "cultural neutrality" — for seeing ourselves as no better than anybody else.

This doesn't really sound so bad, but the need for cultural neutrality can be so well-ingrained or thoroughly done that it causes a willful blindness that overrides common sense and even the basic instinct of self-preservation. It has clearly gone off the deep end in some people.

Hanson wrote: "...so strong is the tug of cultural neutrality that it trumps even the revulsion of Western progressives at the...jihadist agenda, with its homophobia, sexism, religious intolerance, and racism."

It is important to clearly understand this perplexing, confusing, exasperating phenomenon we are all running into: The compulsive, undiscriminating reflex to defend Islam and criticize Western countries.

The source of the resistance we're coming up against could be simply this: People feel guilty for having so much more than others, and this prevents them from accepting your legitimate criticisms of Islamic doctrine.

With this understanding, I think we can begin to find more effective ways of educating our fellow non-Muslims on the basic facts about Islam.

HOW TO DISARM GOOD PEOPLE

IN THE BOOK, *The Sociopath Next Door*, Martha Stout says something really interesting. Her book is about normal, everyday sociopaths (also known by the somewhat outdated term, "psychopath"). In other words, the book is not about serial killers, but about the neighbor who drives you crazy, the spouse who seems dedicated to making your life miserable, the cruel, unfeeling boss, etc.

A sociopath is someone who feels no empathy for other human beings. The consequences of this lack are pervasive. These people are, in some ways, not recognizably human. And no known cure for sociopathy has been discovered. It is not caused by upbringing. Therapy only makes them worse.

About two percent of the population is sociopathic, and those who are in a relationship with a sociopath need to understand what makes sociopaths tick. The more you know, the less likely you are to be fooled, used, or destroyed by a sociopath.

But Martha Stout said something applicable to our conversation about Islam. She wrote about the techniques sociopaths use to exploit the people in their lives. Sociopaths *use* people. And there is one technique sociopaths use more than anything else because it works so well with normal people. The ultra-effective weapon they use is to evoke *pity*. Martha Stout wrote:

> The most reliable sign, the most universal behavior of unscrupulous people is not directed, as one might imagine, at our fearfulness. It is, perversely, an appeal to our sympathy.
>
> I first learned this when I was still a graduate student in psychology and had the opportunity to interview a court-referred patient the system had already identified as a "psychopath." He was not violent, preferring instead to swindle people out of their money with elaborate investment scams. Intrigued by this individual and what could possibly motivate him...I asked, "What is important to you in your life? What do you want more than anything else?" I thought he might say "getting money," or "staying out of jail," which were the activities to which he devoted most of his time. Instead, without a moment's hesitation, he replied, "Oh, that's easy. What I like better than anything else is when people feel sorry for me. The thing I really want more than anything else out of life is people's pity."

I was astonished, and more than a little put off. I think I would have liked him better if he had said "staying out of jail," or even "getting money." Also, I was mystified. Why would this man — why would *anyone* — wish to be pitied, let alone wish to be pitied above all other ambitions? I could not imagine. But now, after twenty-five years of listening to victims, I realize there is an excellent reason for the sociopathic fondness for pity. As obvious as the nose on one's face, and just as difficult to see without the help of a mirror, the explanation is that good people will let pathetic individuals get by with murder, so to speak, and therefore any sociopath wishing to continue with his game, whatever it happens to be, should play repeatedly for none other than pity.

More than admiration — more even than fear — pity from good people is *carte blanche*. When we pity, we are, at least for the moment, defenseless, and like so many of the other positive human characteristics that bind us together in groups...our emotional vulnerability when we pity is used against us...

The reason I thought that was interesting and relevant is that pity is one of the most common techniques Islamic supremacists use, and it is the main reason they've been able to get away with as much as they have so far.

They exploit the egalitarian, multiculturalist, good-hearted nature of non-Muslims. They exploit our guilt. They evoke pity and then use our own kindness and our desire to "get along with others" against us.

I was just reading the book, *Tripoli: The United States' First War on Terror*. The ruler of Tripoli had been seizing U.S. merchant ships, adding the ship to his own fleet, keeping the contents of the ship, and selling the captured sailors into slavery.

It was a very lucrative pirating business.

The U.S. wanted Tripoli to stop it, of course. The ruler of Tripoli said, "Sure, we'll stop attacking your ships if you pay us tribute every year."

So for awhile the U.S. went ahead and paid the "protection money" because we were a new country and had no navy to speak of, and we wanted to continue with our overseas trade. But the ruler of Tripoli decided the tribute they'd agreed to wasn't enough, so he demanded more and when he didn't get it, he started seizing U.S. ships again.

Meanwhile, the U.S. was frantically building a navy, and by this time had enough warships to put up a fight, so we did. Suddenly Tripoli's ruler wanted to talk peace. But in the negotiations, the man negotiating on behalf of the ruler asked for a gift of money. The U.S. said no, absolutely not. The U.S. said basically, "You have not been fair in any way and have only acted as our enemy, and no, we will not pay you to stop the fighting."

Then Tripoli's negotiator tried *an appeal to pity:* "But Tripoli is very poor," he whined, "she cannot subsist without the generosity of her friends; give something then on the score of charity."

In this case, Tripoli already had a poor reputation with the Americans, so the pity plea did not work.

But even after the U.S. negotiator said no, Tripoli's negotiator tried to make the U.S. negotiator feel guilty for not feeling pity. He asked, basically, "You say you want peace but you won't give this gift of charity to obtain the peace?"

Orthodox Islam uses pity and guilt anywhere it can.

Muhammad used it, Muslims in Tripoli were using it, and orthodox Muslims today are still at it. In their dealings with powerful non-Muslims, the basic stance of Islam is: "We are an oppressed, persecuted people. We are a minority. We are under siege. We are wrongly accused. We're the victims of bigotry, hatred, and Islamophobia." And if they can't find anything to point to that proves their oppression, they literally *create* something.

It's like a game they are playing, except this is a game with very serious consequences.

An everyday sociopath using the appeal to pity can completely ruin the lives of several people as the sociopath takes advantage of them. And this is, of course, nothing compared with what Islamic supremacists have done. They've killed over 270 million people since they started. They've *ruined* even more lives, and they are affecting the lives and livelihoods of billions of us today.

I would like to spend my time working on productive, positive, life-affirming activities. Instead, I am spending many hours of my short time here on earth trying to stop this insidious Islamic encroachment, reading and writing about things I wish didn't exist. It's an upsetting topic. It's disturbing. But the consequences of ignoring it are even worse, so I devote a large portion of my life to it.

And, of course, I'm not alone in this. Each of us has been influenced in hundreds of ways we don't even know about by the third jihad (and the first two jihads).

It is important to understand how orthodox Muslims are getting away with it. One of the most successful techniques they use is their appeal to pity. The good news is that as soon as you see the appeal for what it is, the game is over, the magic disappears, the trance is lifted.

Let us together lift the trance of the world and expose Islamic doctrine for what it is. And may all lovers of freedom find our common ground and unite against the encroachment of orthodox Islam.

ABOUT THE AUTHORS

CITIZEN WARRIOR is a blog conceived, written, and published by two people. We were living in almost complete ignorance of the growth or even existence of jihad until September 11th, 2001. But at that time, we were in a unique position to contribute something to our fellow citizens: We were in the middle of a writing project, working on a book specifically aimed at teaching the reader how to recover from the feelings of defeat and demoralization that often come from a setback.

The last thirty-five years of research by cognitive scientists on the causes of depression and anxiety accidentally uncovered something we can call "The Technology of Resilience." That was what our book was going to be about: How to become resilient in the face of setbacks, failures and tragedies.

After September 11th, many people in the United States seemed paralyzed and demoralized. So we started CitizenWarrior.com to do what we could about it.

We wanted to help people prevent themselves from giving up or becoming disheartened. This has been our mission ever since. The site is focused on giving ordinary (non-military) citizens ways to thwart and defeat orthodox Islam's aggressive encroachment around the world.